INSIGHT POCKET GUIDE

RIGa

APA PUBLICATIONS L
Part of the Langenscheidt Publishing Group

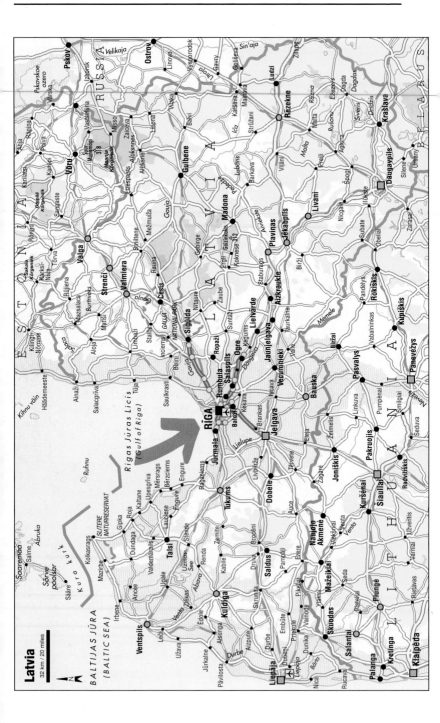

Welcome

This is one of 133 itinerary-based *Pocket Guides* produced by the editors of Insight Guides, whose books have set the standard for visual travel guides since 1970. With top-quality photography and authoritative recommendations, this guidebook is designed to help visitors get the most out of Riga and its surroundings during a short stay. To this end, Martins Zaprauskis, Insight's expert on Latvia, has devised 11 easy-to-follow itineraries linking the essential sights and exploring some hidden gems.

The first four routes focus on Riga's historic city centre and parks, while tours 5 and 6 cover the Art Nouveau and Moscow districts. Route 7 explores the left bank of the river, while the final tour in Riga itself is a trip to Mežaparks, Europe's first garden city. The last three tours suggest excursions beyond the city and include a visit to the beach. There are, in addition, sections on history and culture, eating out, shopping and nightlife, plus a calendar of special events. A detailed practical information section towards the end of the guide covers transport, money matters, communications, etc, and includes reviews of hotels and accommodation options in all price categories.

Martins Zaprauskis first visited Latvia in 1991, shortly after the nation regained its independence. After two weeks of viewing what the Soviets had done to its once-cosmopolitan capital Riga, he vowed never to return. But curiosity got the better of him, and seven years and three scouting trips later he moved to the largest city in the Baltics, where he still edits the highly acclaimed *Riga In Your Pocket* guide. Over the years he has witnessed how his adopted home has grown into a European capital worthy of its 19th-century moniker – the Paris of the North.

HISTORY AND CULTURE

From Riga's founding on the bank of the River Daugava in the early 13th century to the glorious days of the Swedish Empire in the 17th century, Art Nouveau splendour at the turn of the 20th century, the rise and fall of communism, and the city's emergence as a tourist hotspot in the late 20th century – a concise introduction to the history of Latvia's capital **11**

CITY ITINERARIES

These eight itineraries, which can last from a few hours to a full day, cover Riga's most remarkable architectural, historical and cultural treasures.

contents

Preceding pages: view over Riga from St Peter's
Following pages: Livs' Square

History
&Culture

E ven before Riga's founding in 1201, the marshy soil near the bank of the River Daugava was chosen by the native tribes of the land as an ideal base for trade. From its golden era as the greatest city in the Swedish Empire in the 17th century to the eve of World War I, when Riga was Russia's third largest port, it has been the bridge between the vast resources of the East and the hungry markets of the West. Tragically, it wasn't until 1920 that Riga would become the capital of an independent Latvian state – one that had lost infrastructure, industry, a large workforce and countless resources to the war to end all wars. Yet by the 1930s Riga's inhabitants enjoyed one of the highest standards of living in Europe, and their city was dubbed the Paris of the North.

Sadly, larger forces were at play, and Riga was doomed to be the object of conquest by its neighbours, much as it had been for the eight centuries since its inception. After suffering brutal occupations by both the Red Army and the Nazis during World War II, the Pearl of the Baltic would languish behind the Iron Curtain until the collapse of the Soviet Union in 1991. In a relatively short period since independence, however, Riga has pushed once again to the forefront of commerce and culture in the region, reclaiming its rightful place among the great cities of the Baltic Sea. The capital of a nation that is now a member of NATO and the European Union (EU), Riga is finally the master of her own destiny. The city that has relied on its port for its wealth and prosperity has grown accustomed to merchants and invaders over the past 800 years, but it must now contend with the arrival of a new class of visitor – tourists eager to absorb its café culture and admire its UNESCO-protected architecture.

The Crusade

While thousands of zealots and profiteers set sail for the Holy Land, the inhabitants of present-day Northern Germany were presented with another offer. Since the late 12th century, merchants from Bremen, Lübeck and other cities had returned to their homes with tales of prosperous pagans living on the shores of the Baltic Sea to the north. The temptation for wealth and the absolution of sins was apparently too great to pass up, and in 1184 an Augustinian monk named Meinhard arrived at the Liv settlement of Ikšķile on the bank of the River Daugava to convert the infidels.

At the time, Latvia was inhabited by four Baltic tribes – the Semigallians (zemgaļi), the Couronians (kurši), the Selonians (sēļi) and the Letgallians (letgaļi) – and a Finno-Ugric tribe called the Livs who spoke a language similar to Estonian. The fierce tribes were not above fighting among themselves to achieve their aims, so the arrival of foreign interlopers was not at all welcome. Meinhard built a

Left: figure from the banner of the first all-Latvian Song and Dance Festival, 1873. **Right:** World Heritage Site

church and lived amongst the Livs until his death in 1197, but gained few converts. His bloodthirsty successor Berthold believed that he should bring Christianity to the people by any means necessary; he met an ignominious end at the hands of the pagans a year later.

The third bishop of Livonia was far more cunning and ruthless. Albert von Buxhoevden (1165–1229) arrived in 1201 and quickly realised that the trading settlement near the mouth of the River Daugava was strategically sounder and more economically viable than Ikšķile. According to the 13th-century *Chronicle of Heinricus*, Albert invited the local tribesmen to a feast, plying them with alcohol until they were too inebriated to fight the German crusaders who had surrounded them. They grudgingly gave him a parcel of land in return for their lives. Albert began building a fortress there, and Riga was officially born.

Unlike his predecessors, Albert obtained a papal bull from Pope Innocent III to encourage more wayward German peasants to join his mission, which gained the status of an official crusade. In 1202 he also gained permission from Rome to create the Order of the Brotherhood of the Sword, an organisation of monastic warriors not unlike the Knights Templar. A

power struggle began between the Bishop and the Order, and soon the original purpose of supposedly bringing God and civilisation to the heathens was forgotten, as the Germans fought amongst themselves over the lucrative trade routes along the Daugava and the rest of Livonia. By 1210 conquered lands were divided up between the Bishopric of Riga and the Order.

Fierce fighting raged for the rest of the 13th century, and the Livonian Order replaced the Order of the Brotherhood of the Sword, after the latter suffered a crushing defeat at the hands of the Lithuanians and Semigallians when nearly 90 percent of its knights perished. But by 1290, all the Baltic tribes in Livonia had been subjugated.

Over the next two centuries, churches, schools and new fortresses were built, the Riga City Council and the Great Guild were created, and the city joined the prestigious Hanseatic League.

Both political and literal battles continued between the Order, the bishop, the city council and the citizens of Riga, but the Order finally gained the upper hand in 1491.

The End of Teutonic Rule

In 1522 Martin Luther's Reformation arrived in Riga, bringing with it enlightenment and civil unrest. Two years later, a mob of zealous Lutherans stormed the city's churches and monasteries, destroying religious icons and other symbols of Catholicism. The chinks in the Order's armour began to show, and incursions on Livonian lands in the east by Muscovites were taxing the military that had grown fat and complacent. Unable to fight off this new threat, in 1561, the last grandmaster of the Livonian Order swore his allegiance to the king

Above: a knight of the Livonian Order

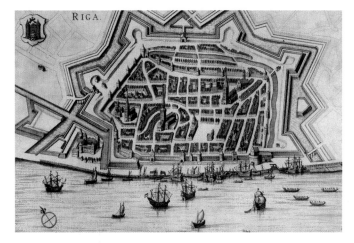

of the Polish-Lithuanian state and was rewarded with the Duchy of Courland in the west. The Order ceased to exist, and Riga enjoyed a short-lived period as a free city until it came under the domination of Poland-Lithuania in 1581.

The Protestant citizens of Riga were dismayed at their city's incorporation into a Catholic kingdom, and enmity rose when it was announced that they were to adopt the Gregorian calendar. Riots broke out, and the city council and guilds attempted to exploit the townspeople's anger to their own ends. Although sporadic disturbances continued for years, by 1600 larger conflicts outweighed local intrigues. Poland would be at war with Sweden for the next three decades, but by 1621 Riga had surrendered to Gustavus Adolphus, king of Sweden.

When Riga became a part of the Swedish Empire it was larger even than the younger capital, Stockholm. The next century was a medieval golden age for Swedish Livonia, when schools and hospitals were built on an unprecedented scale, a practical code of laws was implemented, the first newspaper was published, and the bible was translated into Latvian. The empire at this point was enormous, comprising parts of present-day northern Germany, Poland and Russia, Finland, Estonia and much of Latvia. However, its monopoly on trade in the Baltic Sea was contested by the Muscovites (Russians), who declared war on Sweden in 1656. The tsar's troops laid siege to Riga but eventually lost the stomach for battle and began to desert en masse. Riga's garrison mounted a counterattack, and the defeated Muscovites relinquished all captured Livonian lands to the Swedes. Relative peace and prosperity continued for another four decades, until a more formidable foe acceded to the throne of Moscow.

The Ascendancy of Russia

Peter the Great was determined to break the Swedish stranglehold on the Baltic Sea and began hatching plans to seize Riga as early as 1697, when he visited the city incognito. Four years later, Saxon forces allied with Russia attacked the city, but their efforts were thwarted. However, by 1709 the tables had turned, and the Russian tsar had completely encircled Riga, firing the first cannonball himself. After ten months of siege the effects of starvation and plague forced the citizens of Riga to capitulate.

Above: Riga and the River Daugava, a copperplate engraving from 1638

The Great Northern War finally ended in 1721, and Sweden lost much of its territory, including Livonia. By 1795 the Duchy of Courland was part of the Russian Empire, with all Latvian territory belonging to Russia. This was the darkest period in the history of the Latvian nation. The countryside had been ravaged by plague and war, and serfs who had had rights under the Swedes became little more than slaves.

The Latvian Awakening

The 19th century was a time of revolutionary change in Riga. Serfdom had been abolished by 1819, but Latvian peasants were still prohibited from owning land and so many moved to the city in the hope of finding work and a better life. Although Riga was nominally part of Russia, polite society and business interests were dominated by Baltic Germans – descendants of the original crusaders. Eventually ownership rights were granted to Latvians in the mid-century, and a small Latvian intelligentsia began to emerge. By 1868 the Riga Latvian Society was created to combat the superiority of German culture in Riga. The organisation sponsored the publishing of

Latvian literature, concerts by Latvian musicians and, in 1873, the first Latvian Song and Dance Festival.

Meanwhile the archaic law against the construction of brick buildings outside the city walls was lifted, and a construction boom began. Old Riga's fortifications, which were made obsolete by modern warfare and technology, were torn down and the no-man's land just beyond was transformed into the lush parkland that is still visible today.

The 20th Century

On the eve of World War I Riga had never been so prosperous. It was the third largest port in the Russian Empire and a major railway junction connecting the eastern hinterland with the rest of Europe. A time of unprecedented wealth and optimism heralded the construction of the city's greatest treasures – ornate Art Nouveau buildings. But not all was well in the empire, as the failed 1905 Revolution, which engulfed Riga, had proven. The gap between the haves and have-nots had become enormous, yet when the Germans sped towards Riga in 1915, thousands of Latvians joined the tsar's army to defend their homeland. The fierce *Strēlnieki* (Riflemen), as they were known, held off the invaders for nearly two years, but despite their best efforts, the city was taken. In the November of the following year Germany capitulated, and a group of Latvian intellectuals formed a fledgling government, declaring their independence from foreign powers.

The war had ended for much of Europe, but battles still raged in the east. The Bolsheviks attacked Latvia, seizing Riga in 1919, when a bloody reign of terror began. The Latvian government escaped to Liepāja, but renegade Germans deposed its leader Kārlis Ulmanis, and they fled out to sea protected by British gunships. The Germans installed a puppet government and raised an army that fought the Bolsheviks, pitting brother against brother. Mean-

Above: traditional 'Letttish' costume, 1920s. **Top right:** Latvian infantrymen march through German-occupied Riga. **Right:** Riga inhabitants welcome Red Army soldiers

while, the true Latvian government created its own army, which beat back the Germans with the help of Estonian troops in the north. By 1920 all foreign invaders were expelled from the new Republic of Latvia.

Democracy flourished until 1934, when Ulmanis, one of the founding fathers of the nation, became frustrated with the in-fighting and rivalries in parliament and staged a bloodless coup. Although he was hardly the portrait of a typical dictator, the press was suppressed under his regime, and many industries were nationalised. Yet most Latvians who lived during this period will claim that the Ulmanis years were the best the country had ever seen.

Latvia's brief experiment with sovereignty came to an abrupt end when the Red Army invaded in 1940. Property was seized, and sham elections were held offering only communist candidates. Repressions began, and tens of thousands of people were deported to Siberia in cattle cars to die. Not surprisingly, after a year of torture, executions and deportations, the Latvians welcomed their liberation by the Nazis, who began their own brutal repressions against the local population. Most of Latvia's Jews were executed or perished in concentration camps over the next three years. In 1945 the Nazis were defeated, and the Soviets once again occupied Latvia, annexing it to the USSR, while the Western powers looked on impotently.

Further mass deportations of intellectuals, farmers and any persons deemed a threat to the Soviet state were carried out, the largest of which occurred in March of 1949, when 42,000 men, women and children were herded into cattle cars and deported to a horrible end in Siberia. All attempts to cultivate Latvian language and culture were brutally suppressed, and Russian-speakers from across the Soviet Union were offered jobs in a conscious effort to dilute the ethnic Latvian population. The effects of these policies were so devastating that on the eve of regaining independence Latvians had nearly become a minority in their own nation.

But cracks in the communist citadel began appearing when Mikhail Gorbachev's *glasnost* and *perestroika* initiatives allowed the masses to speak their

minds. Local grass roots organisations, originally designed to improve Latvia's catastrophic environmental record, evolved into political forces that organised demonstrations on a scale never before witnessed in the Soviet Union.

By 1990 all three of the captive Baltic nations declared their independence, stipulating a period of transition. But a brutal crackdown in the Lithuanian capital of Vilnius in January of 1991, during which over a dozen people were killed, convinced Latvians from across the country to defend the parliament from tanks by erecting makeshift barricades. In August of the same year a coup against the government failed in Moscow, and Latvia declared its complete independence from the USSR.

Latvia joined the United Nations soon after, with its first free post-Soviet elections held in 1993. The last Russian troops withdrew from the country in 1994, and Latvia's democratically elected representatives set a bold agenda that included membership of both NATO and the EU – objectives achieved in 2004.

City of Inspiration

There's no doubt that war and commerce have shaped the landscape of Riga, but the ancient fortress city and its bustling port have also been fertile ground for art, literature and, especially, music. The economic juggernaut of the Baltic Sea has also been home to world-renowned luminaries of ballet such as native son Mikhail Baryshnikov. Lucrative trade provided untold wealth for the city, but this prosperity is also responsible for the creation of the largest organ the world had yet seen; an instrument so grand that Franz Liszt composed music in its honour. Riga's uncompromising money lenders eventually caused the troubled composer Richard Wagner to flee the city in 1839, but not before he wrote *Oh Tannenbaum*, a song sung around the world each Christmas. His fearful flight on the stormy seas of the Baltic inspired him to write the *Flying Dutchman*, one of his most enduring works.

It is then no coincidence that Riga refers to itself as the City of Inspiration. Its long history of cultural innovation continues to this day at the opera and several theatres throughout the city that hold sold out performances for an enthusiastic public. Hardly traditional, local theatre and opera is often praised as groundbreaking and what it may lack in funding, it more than makes up for in originality. This search for new possibilities is a fundamental part of Riga's spirit and evident in the works of its contemporary musicians, including the violin virtuoso Gidon Kremer who was born in the Latvian capital in 1947.

The citizens of Riga respect the city's illustrious past but are hungry for change and opportunity. A local legend claims that from time to time a voice asks from the depths of the River Daugava whether or not the city is finished. If a passer-by answers 'yes', the city will collapse into the dark blue waters from whence it came – a harsh penalty for complacency. Perhaps this is the reason that Riga is never willing to rest on its laurels, cultural or economic.

Above: protesters near the Riga parliament

HISTORY HIGHLIGHTS

2500BC The ancestors of modern Latvians arrive on the Baltic Sea.

1100s German merchants begin trading with Latvian and Liv tribes.

1201 Bishop Albert founds Riga.

1202 The pope approves the creation of the Livonian Order in Riga.

1282 Riga joins the Hanseatic League.

1290 German crusaders subdue the last of the Latvian tribal kingdoms.

1300–1500 The town council, the bishop and the Order fight for control of the city.

1522 The Reformation arrives in Riga, bringing with it social unrest.

1561 The last grand master of the Livonian Order pledges allegiance to the Polish king and the Order ceases to exist.

1584–89 The introduction of the Gregorian calendar sparks riots in fiercely Lutheran Riga, which the guilds and town hall exploit to their own ends.

1600 The Polish-Swedish war begins.

1621 Riga surrenders to the king of Sweden, heralding a golden age.

1700 The Great Northern War begins between the Russian and Swedish empires.

1710 The Russian tsar Peter the Great conquers Riga.

1817–19 Serfdom is abolished.

1873 The first Latvian Song Festival is held in Riga.

1905 The 1905 revolution fails and hundreds are executed in Riga.

1915 Riflemen are recruited to defend what is now Latvia from the Germans.

1917 Riga falls to an advancing German army.

1918 Latvian independence is finally proclaimed by the Latvian National Council.

1919 Russian Red Army forces take Riga, and the Latvian government flees to Liepāja.

1921 Renegade German forces are driven out of Latvia and the Soviets sign a peace treaty.

1934 Kārlis Ulmanis executes a bloodless coup and becomes the benevolent dictator of Latvia.

1940 The Soviet Union invades Latvia.

1941 The Nazis drive out the Soviets and the Holocaust begins in Latvia.

1944 The Red Army once again occupies most of Latvia.

1945 The war ends and Latvia is left behind the Iron Curtain.

1986 The independence movement begins with public demonstrations.

1988 The Latvian People's Front is established to further the cause of independence.

1989 Approximately 2 million Latvians, Lithuanians and Estonians join hands in the Baltic Way protest, which stretches from Vilnius to Tallinn.

1991 Soviet troops open fire in Riga. The August coup fails in Moscow and Latvia declares its independence. The USSR recognises the independence of Latvia and it is admitted to the UN.

1993 The first free post-Soviet elections in nearly 60 years take place. Guntis Ulmanis, leader of the Latvian Peasants' Union (LZS), is elected as president.

1994 The last Soviet troops withdraw from Latvia.

1996 Elections take place. Ulmanis is re-elected.

1999 Latvia's first female president, Vaira Vīķe-Freiberga, is elected.

2001 The city of Riga celebrates its 800th anniversary.

2002 The EU passes the official vote to invite Latvia to join it in 2004.

2003 The Eurovision Song Contest is hosted by Riga.

2004 Latvia joins NATO and the European Union.

history/culture

Central Riga

400 m / 437 yds

Orientation

Riga may be the largest city in the Baltic States, but it's surprisingly compact. Nearly all sights of merit can be reached on foot or by a short trip by tram or trolleybus. The following eight itineraries explore Riga's most remarkable architectural and historical treasures. Discover the medieval splendour of the old town and the Art Nouveau gallery of the city centre, or the lesser known, yet equally impressive, heritage of the unique 19th- and early 20th-century neighbourhoods of Mežaparks, Europe's first garden city, and the Moscow District, whose faded glory still fails to disappoint. Walk along the canal and its perfectly manicured gardens or venture across the river to see the Left Bank's Soviet legacy. The scenic towns of Jūrmala, Sigulda and Bauska, covered in a further three itineraries, are all just a short ride from the Latvian capital and make for excellent day trips.

City Layout and Opening Hours

Orientation is fairly simple, if you bear in mind a few general rules of thumb. The old town is nearly entirely encircled by a canal, which separates it from the more modern grid-like streets of the city centre. The River Daugava acts as a natural border on the other side of Old Riga, and two main bridges – the harp-like Vanšu tilts and the Akmens tilts, decorated with giant street lamps – connect it to the Left Bank (or Pārdaugava). Furthermore, the pedestrian Kaļķu iela divides the old town into nearly equal halves. The imposing black spire of the Doma baznīca (Dome Cathedral) and its sprawling cobbled square is the focal point of the northern half of the old town, while the taller green copper spire of Pēterbaznīca (St Peter's Church) is an easy landmark to remember in the southern half of Riga's old town.

By western standards, entrance fees to museums are ridiculously inexpensive, but bear in mind that opening hours are often prohibitively short. Many seasoned tourists are often disappointed to discover that museums have yet to open their doors at 10am, and that major attractions are closed on both Mondays and Tuesdays. Likewise, numerous churches, including the massive Dome Cathedral, keep odd hours and may bar entrance to tourists during religious services. Thankfully, Riga has yet to become a European tourist Mecca, therefore queues are seldom seen at any sights in the city, with the exception of the lift to the observation deck of St Peter's.

Left: looking down from St Peter's spire
Right: Freedom Monument

1. NORTHERN OLD RIGA *(see map p24)*

This is the first of two essential tours that will acquaint you with the medieval architecture of Old Riga, a UNESCO World Heritage Site. The 13th-century Dome Cathedral and crusader castle are just two of its many historic sights.

Seven streets end at **Doma laukums** (Dome Square), the heart and soul of Old Riga, yet curiously much of this empty cobbled expanse lay beneath ancient apartment buildings only a century ago. Some of these buildings were demolished at the beginning of the 20th century to grant greater access to the cathedral; the rest were reduced to rubble by Soviet bombs at the close of World War II. If you look closely at the patterns of the cobblestones, the original streets can be discerned. At the centre of the square is a bronze disk *(see page 11)* that commemorates the old town's inclusion in UNESCO's World Heritage list; it also marks the spot from which you can see four church spires.

Jauniela and Palasta Streets

We'll return to the square shortly, but first head down Jauniela, the scenic street to the left of the cathedral. On your left is the **1991 Barikāču muzejs** (1991 Barricades Museum; Krāmu 3; tel: 721 35 25; open Mon–Fri 10am–5pm, Sat 11am–5pm; free), worth a quick peek if you're interested in how Latvia regained its independence in 1991. The museum is dedicated to the Latvians who came from across the country to protect the parliament from Soviet forces by erecting makeshift barricades.

Nos 25–29 Jauniela is one of Old Riga's best examples of Art Nouveau architecture. Built in 1903, its massive 53-m (174-ft) long façade is divided into three distinct parts to better

Above: bird's-eye view over Dome Square
Left: the cathedral's original copper weathervane

city itineraries

fit into its medieval surroundings of narrow buildings. Its most distinctive feature is a massive head with a sun behind it. Across the street, in the small courtyard of Nos 18–22, are several **tombstones** that once paved the floor of Dome Cathedral. To the left, in the corner, is a small relief of the crucifixion of Christ that is believed to have once adorned the interior of the church. If you look down beyond the iron gate you can see the original height of the city before centuries of construction, fires and floods took their toll.

At the end of the street on the right, at **No. 9 Palasta**, is the former palace of Peter the Great. The 17th-century building, which has been reconstructed on no less than three occasions, was presented as a gift to the conquering tsar, who visited the city often. Over the years it played host to European royalty including Catherine the Great. Further down Palasta on the right-hand side is perhaps the only medieval carriage house in existence in Riga. It's rumoured that Peter the Great kept his coach here.

Just ahead on the right is the entrance to one of the city's most eclectic museums, **Rīgas vēstures un kuģniecības muzejs** (Museum of Riga's History and Navigation; Palasta 4; tel: 735 66 76; open Wed–Sun 11am–5pm; admission fee). In operation since 1773, and moved to this spot in 1891, it is also one of Riga's oldest museums. Exhibits document the area's history from the Bronze Age to the 20th century, and among the artefacts are ancient weapons, suits of armour, the sword of the Riga executioner and the mummified hand of an unfortunate thief. Paintings and memorabilia from the inter-war period are also displayed.

Next door is the entrance to **Doma krusteja** (Dome Cloister; Palasta 4; tel: 721 13 58; open daily May 1– October 1 10am–5pm; admission fee), considered to be the most spectacular example of Romanesque architecture in the Baltics and, at 118m (387ft), the longest cloister in Northern Europe. The beautiful arches are in need of renovation, as is the courtyard, but it's still worth a quick look. Cumbersome bits and pieces of Riga's history are also on display here, including the cathedral's original copper weathervane (dating to 1595), ancient tombs from the 13th to 18th centuries, a giant carved rock believed to be an ancient pagan idol, and an 11th-century stone baptismal font from the first church built on Latvian soil.

Herder Square and the Cathedral

Exit the cloister onto **Herdera laukums** (Herder Square), named in honour of the eminent German philosopher Johann Gotfried Herder (1744–1803), who once taught at the Dome school. A bust of the influential thinker is located in the centre of the square. Head towards the imposing doors of **Doma baznīca** (Dome Cathedral; tel: 735 66 99; open Tues–Fri 11am–4pm, Sat 10am–2pm; admission fee), the largest house of worship in the Baltics. Ground was consecrated for the church as early as 1211, but it would undergo several different periods of construction spanning eight centuries – which accounts for the various styles evident in its exterior and interior, namely Romanesque, Baroque, early Gothic and even a touch of Art Nouveau. The cathedral adopted its current appearance in the 18th century after it was seriously damaged in a fire. Its characteristic steeple was destroyed by lightning strikes on a number of occasions but the 90-m (295-ft) tall one you see today dates back to 1776. Sadly, many of the building's lavish decorations were destroyed during the riots that followed the introduction of Luther's Reformation in the 1520s – and once again by the Soviets, who used the church as a concert hall.

The cathedral still hosts frequent concerts with performers from around the globe, who often waive their fees for the opportunity to play on the magnificent **organ**, one of the largest in Europe. The original organ was built in the late 16th century and included fantastic woodcarvings by some of the best artists of the day. By the 19th century the congregation decided to replace it with a new one, and a fundraising campaign was begun, garnering donations

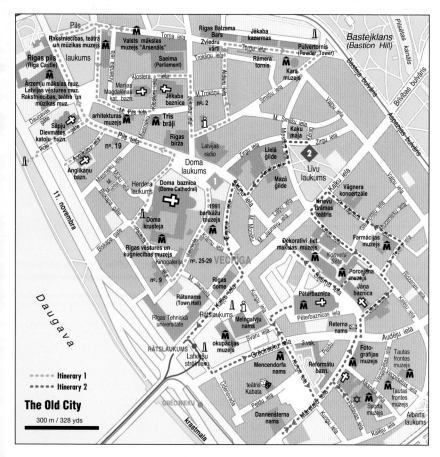

The Old City
300 m / 328 yds

from even the tsar himself. The best firm in Europe, Walcker and Co. of Ludwigsburg, was hired, producing a masterpiece that featured 124 registers and four manuals made from over 6,700 wooden and metal pipes. This made the instrument the world's largest at the time. Its inauguration in 1884 was such an event that Franz Liszt composed music in its honour. All of the original medieval woodcarvings were preserved and can be viewed to this day.

Around Cathedral Square

After a tour of the building, head out onto Cathedral Square. In the summer, café terraces fill the area, and it's a great place to stop for food and a local brew. The green-and-brown Venetian Renaissance edifice at No. 6 is home to **Rīgas birža** (Riga Stock Exchange), completed in 1855 in a style chosen to reflect the building's mercantile function.

Further down Pils iela – on the left at **No. 11** – is another original building, which has links with trade and commerce and served as a club for wealthy English, Scottish and Irish merchants. Although it now serves as the Danish embassy, reliefs of a rose, thistle and shamrock on its façade are poignant reminders of its original purpose.

At the end of Anglikāņu iela is yet another glimpse of British influence in Riga – **Anglikāņu baznīca** (St Saviour's). Built on consecrated earth imported from England in 1857, the neo-Gothic red-brick church still offers religious services in English to the city's growing expatriate community, just as it did in the 19th century.

At the end of Pils iela, at No. 5, is **Sāpju Dievmātes katoļu baznīca** (Church of Our Lady of Sorrow), a sky-blue church with an interesting history. While passing through Riga on his way to St Petersburg, the Austrian Emperor Kaiser Joseph II noticed the pathetic wooden church that once stood here. A devout Catholic, he took it upon himself to build a better place of worship for the local members of his faith. However, things would end badly for him and for all other royalty involved in the project – the Kaiser died a laughing stock in his native land, and anarchists blew up Tsar Alexander II, who also donated money to the church. The building was completed in 1785.

Castle Square

In case you didn't notice the massive yellow structure in front of you, you're now on **Pils laukums** (Castle Square). If you'd like to take a stroll along the river, then head down Poļu gāte and carefully cross the highway at the pedestrian crossing. The first thing you'll notice is a large wooden statue encased in glass by the promenade. This is a replica of **Lielais Kristaps** (Big Christopher), which first appeared on the

Right: Riga Stock Exchange

right bank of the Daugava in the 16th century. Legend has it that the giant once carried the Christ child across the river and was rewarded with a treasure of gold with which he built the city. Riga's citizens used to leave offerings to Christopher before embarking on a journey, and he is considered to be the protector of the city against floods and other natural disasters. The original statue is kept in the Museum of Riga's History and Navigation *(see page 23)*.

Riga Castle

Rīgas Pils (Riga Castle; Pils 3) was built at its present location in 1330, after the original fortress of the Order of the Brothers of the Sword was destroyed by an angry mob of townspeople. It was destroyed once again by Riga's inhabitants in the 15th century and wasn't rebuilt until 1515. It served as the home of the much-hated knights of the Livonian Order until 1561, when the order was disbanded. Redesigned and renovated over the centuries, it still retains its original square fortress shape. Today, it houses the offices of the Latvian president, so much of the building is closed to the public. There are, however, two museums inside, and it's worth the low entrance fee to these just to get a closer look at the castle interior.

Ārzemju mākslas muzejs (Museum of Foreign Art; Pils 3; tel: 722 64 67; open Tues–Sun 11am–5pm; admission fee; www.amm.lv) is home to a large collection of exhibits from ancient Egypt to 20th-century Western Europe,

including sculptures, paintings and tapestries. Many of the works were donated in the last two centuries by wealthy Rigans.

Latvijas vēstures muzejs (Museum of Latvian History; Pils 3; tel: 722 30 04; open Wed–Sun 11am–5pm; admission fee) offers visitors a view of the evolution of Latvia, from Stone-Age artefacts to 20th-century furniture.

If you'd like to visit another museum, walk down Torņa iela at the far end of Pils laukums to **Valsts mākslas muzejs 'Arsenāls'** (Arsenal National Art Museum; Torņa 1; tel: 721 36 95; open Tues–Sun 11am–5pm; admission fee), which offers frequent temporary exhibitions of contemporary local and foreign art as well as permanent exhibits of 20th-century Latvian artists' works, including those of Latvians living abroad.

Three Brothers

From the square proceed down Mazā Pils iela until you reach the ensemble of medieval buildings at Nos 17, 19 and 21, often referred to as **Trīs brāļi** (Three Brothers). The oldest surviving residential buildings in Riga, they were constructed at least a century apart from one another, and each represents a different style of architecture. The oldest is No. 17 on the far right (as you face them) and dates back to the 15th century, while

Top: Riga Castle. **Left:** Parliament detail. **Right:** Three Brothers

No. 21 on the left was built in the 18th century and is the most recent. No. 19 was built in the 17th century and houses **Latvijas arhitektūras muzejs** (Latvian Architecture Museum; tel: 722 07 79; open Mon–Fri 10am–6pm; free). The exhibits here may prove too academic for the non-architect, but the museum is worth a visit to see the interior of the building.

St Jacob's and Parliament

Turn left on Klostera iela and walk to the entrance portal of **Jēkaba baznīca** (St Jacob's Church; tel: 732 64 19; open daily 9am–7pm; free), which bears the inscription 'Anno 1225'. Ironically, the church that is now the largest Catholic house of worship in the city was the first in Riga to hold a Protestant service back in 1522. It is also the only church in the city to retain a Gothic steeple – made more unusual by the fact that its bell is on its exterior. The original bell bore the telling inscription of 'God please save us from Russians, floods and plague', giving us an insight into the concerns of medieval Rigans. A graffitied concrete slab that once served as part of the 1991 barricades is displayed on the lawn at the opposite end of the church.

Next door is the Latvian parliament, known as **Saeima**. Built in 1863 to resemble a Florentine Renaissance palace, it was originally known as the House of Knighthood and intended as a meeting place and social club for wealthy aristocrats descended from the original German crusaders. It is perhaps fitting that it now serves as the democratic legislature for the very people its builders tried to oppress.

Turn right on Jēkaba iela and head back towards Dome Square, turning left into Smilšu iela. The Art Nouveau masterpiece at **No. 2** was designed

city itineraries

by illustrious Latvian architect Konstantīns Pēkšēns and built in 1902. It is an excellent example of biological romanticism and features large stylised windows crowned with smiling human heads, a central peacock relief – one of the symbols of Art Nouveau – and two human figures whose legs gradually turn into tree trunks. Just ahead, at **No. 8**, is another classic example of Art Nouveau architecture, adorned with nude women and reliefs of stylised faces. Also built in 1902, it was restored to its former glory only recently and is now an office building. Its entrance hall on Aldaru iela is covered in elaborate frescoes.

Around the Swedish Gate

At the end of Aldaru iela is **Trokšnu iela** (Noise Street), one of the prettiest streets in Old Riga. Its ancient name, however, betrays its notorious past as the former locale of medieval bars and brothels that witnessed debauchery on a grand scale and countless brawls. **Zviedru vārti** (Swedish Gate) is directly in front of you. The only gate from the original fortifications still in existence, it was built to commemorate the inclusion of Riga into the Swedish Empire in the 17th century, and the king's symbol, the lion, is still visible. Eerily, the Riga executioner once lived above the gate and used to place a red rose on the windowsill before a beheading.

On the other side of the gate are **Jēkaba kazarmas** (Jacob's Barracks), home to some of Riga's trendiest shops and cafés, not to mention luxury apartments for wealthy locals and foreign dignitaries such as the American ambassador. The long line of buildings was constructed during the 18th century to house soldiers and served that purpose until as recently as 1990. To the left is **Rīgas Balzama bārs** (Torņa 4; tel: 721 44 94; open Sun–Thur 8.30am–midnight, Fri–Sat 8.30am–1am), the perfect place to unwind with the national drink, Rēgas Balzams. The black bitter herbal liquor is served here in a variety of ways, but it is best enjoyed mixed with blackcurrant juice. A wide variety of international cuisine is also available.

Opposite the barracks are the remnants of the **fortress walls** and the **Rāmertornis** guard tower. Although the edifice is impressive from a dis-

Above: architectural detail, Smilšu iela

tance, close scrutiny will reveal modern bricks that betray their youth – Polish experts reconstructed the walls and tower in the 1970s.

At the end of the street is the impressive **Pulvertornis** (Powder Tower), which has stood on the same spot since the early 14th century. First dubbed the sand tower, it was renamed after it was used to store gunpowder in the 1500s. Much of the tower was destroyed during a Swedish bombardment in 1621, but you can see the original stone foundation. It was rebuilt in 1650 with 3-m (10-ft) thick walls, which are now adorned with Russian cannonballs that failed to penetrate it during the 1710 siege of Riga. Today, it is part of **Kara muzejs** (War Museum; Smilšu 20; tel: 722 81 47; open Wed–Sun 10am–6pm; free; www.karamuzejs.lv), which documents the history of the Latvian army from its inception to the present day.

2. SOUTHERN OLD RIGA *(see map p24)*

The second tour of Old Riga takes in some of its most scenic streets, as well as 13th-century churches and ancient buildings, such as the Blackheads' House, that have risen from the ashes of World War II destruction.

Līvu laukums (Livs' Square) is arguably Riga's most popular square and one of Europe's prettiest, yet it did not exist prior to World War II. Once characterised by tall medieval buildings and narrow cobblestone streets, the historic neighbourhood was completely levelled by bombing raids. In the summer the scenic space bristles with activity, as locals and tourists alike people-watch from beer gardens, buskers perform for tips, and souvenir stalls slow the pace of pedestrian traffic. Once called the Philharmonic Square, it was recently renamed in honour of Riga's earliest inhabitants, the Livs, a Finno-Ugric tribe who spoke a language similar to Estonian.

Cats and Guilds

At the northern end of the square is a yellow Art Nouveau building, dating from 1909 and often referred to by locals as **Kaķu māja** (Cat House). The two felines perched on top of its towers are the reason for this memorable moniker. Local lore has it that the owner of the building was refused membership of the prestigious Great Guild across the street and, as revenge, he turned the cats around with their backsides facing the ancient institution of wealth and power. After many insults and negotiations the innocent felines were returned to their original positions, and the owner was admitted to the guild.

Above: around the Swedish Gate
Right: crowning glory of Cat House

The members of **Lielā ģilde** (Great Guild) were among the city's most prosperous German merchants, and for many years the elite few that met here wielded considerable power in Riga. The current neo-Gothic structure dating back to the 1850s was built on top of a much more ancient guildhall from the 14th century. Fortunately, some of its most historic meeting rooms, including the Munster Hall (1330) and the Bride's Chamber (1521), have survived. The building is now home to the Latvian Philharmonic Orchestra.

Although not as large as its imposing neighbour, **Mazā ģilde** (Small Guild) is architecturally more impressive, with a fairytale tower and one of the city's most beautiful neo-Gothic façades. Slightly less prestigious than the Great Guild, members of the Small Guild were the city's skilled craftsmen, who worked for wages. Erected in 1864, their guildhall was completely renovated in 2000 and is currently used for concerts and special events. It also houses the Chamber of Latvian Craftsmen that sells its wares on the premises.

Historic Streets

Walk down Amatu iela (Craftsmen's Street), turning right on Šķūņu iela (Barn Street) and then left onto Tirgoņu iela (Merchants' Street). Each of these streets, like many others in Old Riga, have retained their original, albeit Latvianised, names, indicating the purpose of the locale. Tirgoņu iela is always

abuzz with activity and it offers picturesque views of medieval buildings and some great restaurants and cafés. **Alus Sēta** (Tirgoņu 6; tel: 722 24 31; open daily 10am–1am), literally the Beer Yard, is a great place to take a break with Latvia's tastiest brew, *Užavas*, and some traditional Latvian food such as grey peas with bacon and onions. Further up the street on the right is **Krāmu iela** (Rubbish Street), which has one of the most beautiful views of Dome Cathedral in Riga. It's a favourite stop for photographers and never fails to impress.

Above: Blackheads' House
Left: details of Blackheads' House

Town Hall Square

Just ahead is the reconstructed **Rātslaukums** (Town Hall Square). For centuries this was the heart of the city, where a market was held on weekends, where criminals were humiliated in front of their peers, and where witches were burned at the stake for their 'sins'. At its centre was the **statue of Roland**, Charlemagne's favourite nephew, who died a courageous death in the battle of Roncesvals in 778 and who came to symbolise freedom and justice in many Hanseatic cities in Northern Europe. In the opening days of World War II most of the square and its historic buildings were sadly destroyed, yet, miraculously, the statue of Roland survived. The original is now on display in St Peter's Church, while a replica occupies its original position on the square.

After the war, the ruins of the ancient buildings were bulldozed, and ugly Soviet concrete edifices replaced them, but in the end the citizens of Riga had their way. It was agreed that in honour of the city's 800th anniversary in 2001, the historic square would be returned to its original splendour. The first building to be rebuilt was the mysteriously named **Melngalvju nams** (Blackheads' House; Rātslaukums 7; tel: 704 43 00; open Tues–Sun 10am–5pm; admission fee). Built in 1344 as a guildhall for unmarried travelling merchants of various ethnicities, it soon became synonymous with the bacchanalian exploits of its members, who threw wild parties that were often attended in secret by European royalty. It is unclear whether or not their curious name is derived from their patron saint, the Moor St Mauritius, or from the dark caps they wore, but it is certain that they were a force to be reckoned with in medieval Riga. They were also responsible for the first decorated Christmas tree in Europe, and a bronze disk marks the spot where the no doubt inebriated guildsmen adorned a fir tree with roses and then set it on fire in 1510. The Gothic building with a gabled Dutch Renaissance façade is now open to the public.

The **Rātsnams** (Town Hall) was also rebuilt with an extra storey to accommodate its function as the new home of Riga City Council. The original building dating back to the 14th century was torn down to make room for a much larger structure in 1750. Some 21st-century builders made a curious discovery while excavating its foundations – a 3,500-year-old oak tree is now on display in the subterranean shopping street under the building, with a small plaque that states that the tree grew near the banks of the River Daugava when Tutankhamun was pharaoh of Egypt.

Museum of Occupation

At the far end of the square is an ugly black box that looks like it has no place among the surrounding medieval-style buildings. Appropriately, it houses **Okupācijas muzejs** (Museum of the Occupation of Latvia; Strēlnieku laukums 1; tel: 721 27 15; open daily

Right: Museum of the Occupation of Latvia

May 1– Sept 30 11am–6pm, October 1–April 30 Tues–Sun 11am–5pm; free; www.occupationmuseum.lv). Inside, visitors will discover how the Soviets and Nazis stripped Latvia of its sovereignty and condemned hundreds of thousands of people to torture, execution or death in Siberia. Moving artefacts such has home-made chess sets and instruments donated by survivors of the gulag are on display, as well as a model of a typical barracks in a Soviet prison camp. If you only visit one museum in Riga, make it this one.

Outside is a controversial granite statue of the **Latviešu strēlnieki** (Latvian Riflemen). Originally put up in honour of the Latvian soldiers who joined the Reds after the Russian Revolution, it is now dedicated to all the local troops who joined the tsar's army in 1915. Although some soldiers joined the communists in 1917, a few even becoming the elite guard of Lenin and the rumoured executioners of the Romanovs, others eventually fought for the fledgling Latvian state that declared its independence a year later. In any event, it's an impressive monument.

St Peter's Church

Take the south side of the aptly named Grēcinieku iela (Sinners' Street), home to many of the city's best bars and nightclubs, and turn left into Kungu iela, until you see the weathered limestone sculptures on the façade of **Pēterbaznīca** (St Peter's Church; Skārņu 19; tel: 722 94 26; open Tues–Sun 10am–6pm; admis-

sion fee), one of the symbols of the city. First mentioned in medieval documents in 1209, the church has had a long and tragic history. It was expanded considerably in the 15th century and crowned with a soaring rooster-topped spire in 1491, but this unfortunately proved to be doomed. In 1666 the spire collapsed, killing several passers-by; ten years later, just as repairs were nearing completion, the spire was consumed by fire. In 1690 the new one was finally completed, making St Peter's the tallest wooden structure in Europe at the time, but once again it fell victim to fire and burned to the ground.

Peter the Great, who had witnessed the conflagration, ordered its reconstruction, which was completed in 1746. The architect

Top: inside St Peter's
Left: St Peter's spire

toasted the building with a glass of wine and then dropped the latter to the street below, believing that the number of pieces it broke into would be the number of centuries it would survive. However, a bail of hay broke its fall, and only a small piece was chipped away. Almost exactly 200 years later the spire was hit by a bomb, becoming a towering inferno. Thankfully, the Soviets were persuaded to rebuild the church as a museum, and St Peter's once again rose from the ashes, this time with a metal spire that includes a lift and an observation tower. The glass ritual was repeated in 1973, and the vessel was smashed to bits.

Merchants' Houses

Return to Grēcinieku iela and pay a visit to **Mencendorfa nams** (Mentzendorff's House; Grēcinieku 18; tel: 721 29 51; open Wed–Sun 10am–5pm; admission fee), a museum set in the home of a wealthy 17th-century Riga merchant. Inside you can see how the well-heeled lived in the medieval period and view original period furniture and restored frescoes that languished under layers of Soviet paint.

Now turn right into Kungu and proceed until you reach Mārstaļu iela. To the right, at No. 21, is the neglected shell of **Dannenšterna nams** (Dannenstern House), which once belonged to one of the city's wealthiest medieval merchants. Although the building is badly in need of restoration, its sheer size makes it relatively easy to imagine what it must have looked like in its heyday. Across the street on the opposite side of the car park is one of the few surviving fragments of the **original city walls**. The building that sheltered this piece of history was destroyed during World War II, revealing its ancient treasure.

The Synagogue

Head down Mārstaļu iela in the opposite direction and turn right into Peitavas iela to see the only **synagogue** to have survived the Nazi occupation in Old Riga. Although nearly all other Jewish houses of worship were razed during the Holocaust in Latvia, this one was spared for fear that a fire might spread to neighbouring buildings. The Peitav Shul (Peitavas 6–8; tel: 722 45 48; open daily 10am–4pm; free), as it was known in Yiddish, was constructed in 1905 and has been returned to its Jewish congregation.

Right: Latvian Riflemen

If time allows, the area around the synagogue is worth exploring. Several neglected yet impressive 17th-century warehouses can be seen here, some still with reliefs of a plant or animal above the doorway, indicating what was once stored inside. Many medieval townspeople were illiterate, so a cluster of grapes could be easily understood as wine, while a camel symbolised spices, etc.

Along Mārstaļu

Return to Mārstaļu and proceed until you reach the red Baroque façade of **Reformātu baznīca** (Reformation Church; tel: 721 20 36). Built in 1727, it was converted into a recording studio and youth disco during Soviet times, but has since been returned to its congregation and is open for services. Just ahead is **Latvijas fotogrāfijas muzejs** (Latvian Photography Museum; Mārstaļu 8; tel: 722 72 31; open Tues, Fri–Sat 10am–5pm, Wed–Thur noon– 7pm; admission fee), which traces the evolution of photography in Latvia from 1839 to 1941. Among its best exhibits are the Minox spy cameras once made in Riga and later manufactured under license by the German firm Leica.

At 2–4 Mārstaļu is one of the city's best examples of Baroque architecture. Built in 1684, the former residence of wealthy merchant and politician Johann von Reutern is adorned with long ionic pilasters and a narrow ornamental band featuring a lion pouncing on a bear, signifying the victory of Sweden over Russia. Today the building is used by the Union of Latvian Journalists as an exhibition hall and office space.

Jana Street

From here walk down Skārņu iela (Butchers' Street) towards the green copper neo-Gothic spire of **Jāna baznīca** (St John's Church; Jāņa 7; tel: 722 40 28; open daily 11am–5pm; free). First mentioned in ancient documents in

1297, the church was expanded in 1330, in 1491 and again at the end of the 16th century, when it achieved its current late Gothic appearance. The old spire was replaced by the current one in 1849. The church is said to have excellent acoustics due to its unique net-vaulted ceiling, and is frequently used for concerts. Two medieval monks were immured in the wall facing the street and fed through a small opening, still visible today, by kind-hearted or pious passers-by until their death soon after. Apparently, the clerics did this to achieve sainthood, but were never canonised because they did it for their own glory and not that of God.

At the end of Jāņa iela at **No. 23 Kalēju** is one of the city's most beautiful Art Nouveau buildings.

Left: Riga rooftops

Constructed in 1903 and a fine example of biological romanticism, it now houses a trendy Italian café. At this point, turn left into Kalēju iela (Black-smiths' Street), then first right into Teātra iela. This whole area is currently under construction and will eventually be a large glass-encased shopping atrium – something that has no place in Old Riga and is one of the reasons UNESCO is contemplating revoking Riga's status as a World Heritage Site.

Around the Museum of Pharmacy

Turn left onto R. Vāgnera iela until you reach **Farmācijas muzejs** (Museum of Pharmacy; R. Vāgnera 13; tel: 721 30 08; open Tues–Sat 10am–5pm; admission fee), one of the only buildings in the city with a rococo façade. Porcelain jugs, glass bottles and antique tools of the chemist's craft are all on display here. At the end of the street is the **Vāgnera koncertzāle** (Wagner Concert Hall), named after the illustrious composer Richard Wagner who conducted here from 1837 to 1839. He wrote the music to *Oh Tannenbaum* while living in Riga, and his daring escape from his creditors on the stormy seas of the Baltic served as his inspiration for the *Flying Dutchman*.

Turn left on the square and pass **Krievu drāmas teātris** (Russian Drama Theatre), built by a Russian union as a club and entertainment hall at the end of the 19th century. After World War II it was used as a theatre, and the ugly con-crete addition on the right side is typically Soviet. Note the clever reliefs of beehives on the façade meant to attract bears (Russians). Turn left onto Kalēju and make your way to the brick gate on the right that is the entrance to **Jāna sēta** (St John's Courtyard). It was once a part of the early 13th-century fortress of the Order of the Brotherhood of the Sword and later a monastery, but it was destroyed by angry townspeople in 1297. Today it is home to a few bars and clubs and, in summer, a great beer garden run by the neighbouring hotel.

Ecke's Convent

At the opposite end of the courtyard walk through the gate that was once the entrance to the monastery, into Skārņu iela (Butchers' Street). The lovely early 15th-century yellow building to your right at Nos 20–22, known as **Ekes konvents** (Ecke's Convent), was originally built as accommodation for

Right: stained glass at the Museum of Pharmacy

travellers, but was converted in 1596 into a shelter for indigent widows by Riga mayor Nicolaus Ecke. Although the beautiful Renaissance bas-relief of *Jesus and the Sinner* was later added to the façade in honour of his charitable act, it is believed that the influential politician made the gesture to distract the public from the embezzlement scandal in which he was embroiled. The building now houses a small hotel and a teashop and café. Across the street is a sculpture of the **Bremen town musicians**, based on the fairytale by the Brothers Grimm. It was a gift from the city of Bremen, a Hanseatic sister city and home of Riga's founder, Bishop Albert (1165–1229).

The next gate on Skārņu iela leads to **Konventa sēta** (Convent Yard), a complex of medieval buildings that have been converted into a hotel; there are a few shops and restaurants here too. This is also the site of **Rīgas porcelāna muzejs** (Riga Porcelain Museum; Kalēju 9–11; tel: 750 37 69; open Tues–Sun 11am–6pm; admission fee), which illustrates the development of porcelain manufacturing in the city from the mid-19th century. Among the museum's most notable exhibits are a giant vase commemorating Riga's 700th anniversary and porcelain wares from the Soviet period decorated with portraits of Lenin and Stalin. You can create your own designs with the help of the staff for a mere 3Ls.

Museum of Decorative and Applied Art

A little further up the street is the **Dekoratīvi lietišķas mākslas muzejs** (Museum of Decorative and Applied Art; Skārņu 10–20; tel: 722 78 33; open Tues–Sun 11am–5pm, Wed 11am–7pm; admission fee), housed in what used to be St George's Church, the oldest surviving building in the city. The museum displays Latvian tapestries, porcelain, woodcarvings and other crafts, some of which are for sale.

At the end of the street, at **No. 2 Skārnu**, is one of the city's earliest Art Nouveau buildings, which has the added distinction of having been the home of the famous Jewish-American photographer Philippe Halsman (1906–79), friend of such luminaries as Albert Einstein and Salvador Dalí. This concludes your tour of Old Riga.

Above: St John's Courtyard. **Left:** Bremen town musicians
Right: boating on the canal

3. FREEDOM MONUMENT AND CANAL PARK
(see map p39)

This tour is a stroll along the city's picturesque canal park, beginning with the stunning 19th-century opera house and ending at the iconic Freedom Monument.

For most of its 800-year history, Riga was considered to be a fortress city. It was thought that the city's medieval core could be more easily defended if it was surrounded by wooden structures that could be burned to the ground before an approaching army could use them for shelter or artillery positions. Brick buildings were hence only allowed to be erected within its extensive system of walls and ramparts. However, by the 19th century, modern warfare and weaponry made the old fortifications obsolete; business was booming, and the city's inhabitants were suffocating behind its antiquated walls. The decision was finally made to dismantle the stone, brick and earth constructions that had protected the city for centuries, and the ban against masonry buildings in other districts was lifted.

It was during this time that much of the 'new' centre took shape. A series of parks was created where there had once been a no-man's land, and classic and eclectic-style buildings rose up beside grand boulevards wider than several old town streets. Riga was becoming a modern city, and many of the sights in this tour were constructed during that period.

National Opera

Latvijas Nacionālā opera (Latvian National Opera; Aspazijas bulvāris 3; www.opera.lv), arguably the most beloved building in Riga, was one of the first buildings to be renovated after regaining independence, at an incredible cost to taxpayers and philanthropists alike. The original building, called the First or German Theatre of Riga, was completed in 1863 but it was then destroyed by fire in 1882 due to a gas leak in the lighting system. New con-

struction began a few years later with the addition of an electric power station, whose soaring chimney is still visible. The station generated enough power to light the opera house and nearby city blocks safely, quite a feat, considering the age. The opera's exquisite gilded interior is one of the most spectacular and best preserved in Europe. Luminaries to have begun their careers here include dancer Mikhail Baryshnikov, a native son of Riga.

The attractive **opera gardens** are a favourite place for locals to relax, chat and feed the pigeons. At the centre is a fountain with a bronze sculpture of a nymph holding a clamshell, created in 1887 to celebrate the opening of the new theatre. The surrounding flower beds, lawn and pathways flanked by exotic flora next to the canal are expertly manicured and make for the perfect place from which to admire the massive ionic columns of the opera house and the elaborate frieze above them.

University of Latvia

Cross the canal over the **Timma tilts** (Timm Bridge), a small pedestrian walkway with a history. In his last will and testament, Professor Timm, who worked at the university on the other side of the canal, left his students a final 'gift'. He bequeathed a large sum of money to build a small bridge across the canal, so that his students would no longer have an excuse for being late for lectures. The structure has served as a shortcut for the citizens of Riga and tardy students since 1900.

The building that now houses **Latvijas Universitāte** (University of Latvia) was once home to the Riga Polytechnic Institute. Initial construction was completed in 1869, although other wings were subsequently added, eventually filling the entire block. Its façade is adorned with the coats-of-arms of the three major regions of Baltic Livonia – Livland (Vidzeme), Courland (Kurzeme) and Estland (Estonia) – and its characteristic yellow bricks were imported from England. Its faculty and students were the elite of the day and included Nobel Prize candidates and engineers involved in the building of major projects, such as the Siberian railway and even the Panama Canal. In 1919 the new University of Latvia replaced the polytechnic and it is still the most prestigious institution of higher education in the country.

Top: National Opera House
Above: University of Latvia

Latvia Society House

At the end of Arhitektu on the right side is the **Latviešu biedrības nams** (Latvian Society House), home to one of the most important organisations in the history of Latvia. In an era when many Latvians chose to assimilate into the predominant German society to succeed, the aim of the society was to promote all things Latvian, including language and culture. It published books, organised the first Latvian Song and Dance Festival (in 1873) and was instrumental in the creation of a Latvian national identity. The original structure was built in 1869 and extended over the years until a fire destroyed it at the start of the 20th century. Construction of the current house began within a year. Apart from the granite ionic columns at the entrance, the building's most impressive features are the façade's frescoes, painted by Latvian artist Janis Rozentāls and illustrating various themes from local folklore, legends and myths. The building is open to the public, and the **Senā klēts** (Merķeļa 13; tel: 724 23 98; open Mon–Fri 10am–6pm, Sat 10am–4pm) folklore shop, selling traditional Latvian costumes, tablecloths and souvenirs, is among the best in the city.

Embassy Street

Returning to Raiņa bulvāris you'll no doubt be impressed by the 19th-century buildings on the boulevard, many of which serve as foreign embassies. The peach coloured neo-Gothic edifice at **No. 13** is home to the embassy of the Germans, whose government bought it in 1920. After many years of neglect under the Soviet system, it was finally returned to its German owners after the regaining of Latvian independence and was fully renovated to its present opulent state. Just ahead on the right at **No. 9** is the French Embassy, which has also recently been restored to its former glory. Built in 1872 as a private residence, its façade is covered with the

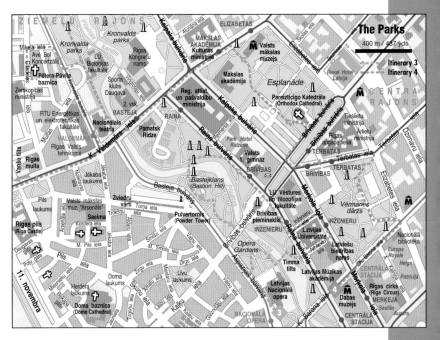

likenesses of 19th-century aristocrats long forgotten. Further down the street, at **No. 7**, behind iron fences and barricades, is the fortress-like American Embassy.

Memorial Stones

Walk across the street and take one of the footpaths along the canal in the direction of the pedestrian bridge. You'll no doubt notice the polished granite slabs that dot the landscape of the park. Each red rock marks the location of a person who was shot by Soviet forces during the civil unrest of January 1991. The **memorial stones**, often strewn with flowers left by the citizens of a grateful nation, can be found on both sides of the canal.

Among the dead were cameramen Gvido Zvaigzne and Andris Slapiņš, who were filming the events for a documentary on the crumbling of the USSR by renowned Latvian director Juris Podnieks. The last managed to escape with only a severe beating, but he died a year later in a suspicious diving accident in a local lake. However, this was not before his films *Is It Easy to Be Young?*, *Homeland* and *Hello, Do You Hear Us?* were praised by critics and fans at home and abroad. Their disturbing footage of Soviet snipers firing on civilians, as seen through the eyes of dying men, were broadcast by most major television media, much to the chagrin of the communists who had hoped that the world would be distracted by the first Gulf War raging in Iraq.

Cross the footbridge and you will have an excellent view of the canal and the only remaining part of the city's original fortifications to the left, where the land juts out into the water at a sharp angle. The bridge itself is usually festooned with locks of various sizes and colours left by Russian couples on their wedding day for good luck. Latvians, on the other hand, carry their brides over as many bridges as possible for the same reason, which is considerably more taxing than the Western tradition of carrying your beloved over the threshold.

Above: locks, traditionally left as love tokens

Bastion Hill

Bastejkalns (Bastion Hill), Riga's second highest hill at a towering 16m (52ft) above sea level, is on the other side of the canal. It may not be tall by European standards, but it did not even exist before the 1860s. When the city's ancient walls and ramparts were demolished, a place in which to store the debris was needed. The creation of a park with a scenic hill at its centre seemed like a logical idea, and Bastion Hill was born.

Several paths lead to the top, which provides excellent views of the surrounding sights in the winter months. During the summer, however, hundred-year-old trees obscure many of the vistas. The park has been remodelled over the years, and some of its fortified slopes are adorned with ancient treasures that became casualties of war. Cannons, limestone busts and other curiosities recovered from damaged buildings following World War II were embedded in its walls for posterity.

Freedom Monument

Walk down the hill to **Brīvības piemineklis** (Freedom Monument), the centrepiece of Riga and hallowed ground for the Latvian nation. Ironically, the very spot occupied by the symbol of Latvian independence once served as the foundation for a giant statue of Peter the Great, the 18th-century subjugator of Latvia. The monumental statue went missing during World War I, and it wasn't until 1935 that the present shrine to freedom was erected.

The monument is dominated by the figure of a woman, colloquially referred to as Milda. She holds three golden stars aloft, each of which represents one of the traditional regions of Latvia – Kurzeme, Vidzeme and Latgale. The base, which is considerably more complex, comprises three different levels. The first bears reliefs of a song festival procession and marching infantry, while the second depicts four central themes – safeguarding the homeland, work, the proletariat and the family. The third and highest level depicts characters from Latvian folklore including Mother Latvia, Lāčplēsis (the Bear Slayer), Vaidelotis and the breakers of chains.

An honour guard, replaced every hour on the hour from 9am–6pm, stands at the foot of the monument. Each day Latvians lay flowers here under the inscription *Tēvzemei un Brīvībai* (For Fatherland and Freedom), an act that would have earned them a trip to the gulag or at least arrest and imprisonment during the Soviet era. The monument was completely renovated in 2001.

Above: reflections near Bastion Hill
Right: on guard at the Freedom Monument

city itineraries

4. CENTRAL PARKS *(see map p39)*

Walk through Riga's finest green spaces and take in some of the city's grandest architecture, including the Orthodox Cathedral, National Art Museum, Academy of Arts and National Theatre.

Old Riga is essentially separated from the new centre by a series of landscaped parks that nearly encircle it. The land directly outside the old city walls was largely undeveloped in the early 19th century for military reasons. Much of the area was divided into small farming plots, and the buildings that did exist were made of wood, as decreed by the tsar. In 1812, a rumour spread that Napoleon's troops were fast approaching Riga, and the order was given to burn the suburbs to rob the enemy of shelter. Unfortunately, the dust cloud of the invading army that had sent people into a panic was in fact that of a herd of cattle. Luckily, the devastation had a silver lining. The inspired Italian governor of the Baltic region, Fillipo di Paulucci, initiated the development of the razed suburbs, and the current design of central parks and boulevards that came about during his stewardship survive to this day.

Museum of Natural History

Begin your tour of the city centre at No. 4 Barona, at **Latvijas dabas muzejs** (Museum of Natural History; open Wed–Sat 10am–5pm, Sun 10am–4pm; admission fee); opened in 1845, it is one of Latvia's oldest museums. Inside you'll find an eclectic collection of flora and fauna from the Cretaceous era to the present day and taxidermied creatures from Latvia and abroad. Among

Above: view over the Orthodox Cathedral and surrounding parks

the museum's most prized possessions is the ancient exhibit of prehistoric fish fossils in the former Soviet Union. Upstairs are odd examples of curiosities swimming in jars of formaldehyde, like an exhibition at a 19th-century freak show. Unfortunately, most of the information is in Latvian, Russian or Latin. If nothing else, the museum is a good place to entertain children.

Riga Circus and Europa Royale Hotel

Another favourite of the young and young at heart is **Rīgas cirks** (Riga Circus), further ahead at the junction of Barona and Merķeļa streets. Originally built in 1889, it is the oldest permanent circus in the Baltics and still dazzles thousands of children each year with death-defying high-wire acts and animal performances. Even before the construction of the current building, an outdoor circus operated on the site, but by 1888 the simple tent became too cramped and was abandoned in favour of the historic edifice you now see. Its unique dome, commissioned by Albert Solomonsky, the P.T. Barnum of the region, is constructed from railway track. The circus is closed in the summer.

The **Europa Royale Hotel** at 12 Barona was originally built as a mansion for a wealthy flax merchant named Pfab in 1876. It was sold, in 1929, to the Benjamiņš family, who had amassed a huge fortune in publishing. Various subjects are depicted among the symbols of the city that adorn the Florentine Renaissance façade, considered to be one of the best examples of the eclectic style that was so popular in mid-19th-century Riga. The original owners paid homage in this way to the foundations of their success, namely the family and the port and train station, without which they would never have risen to such heights.

Wöhrmann Park

Across the street is **Vērmanes dārzs** (Wöhrmann Park), which, since its creation, has been one of Riga's most popular public spaces. After the tragic burning of the suburbs in 1812, Anna Gertrud Wöhrmann donated an area of land to be used as a place of rest and relaxation for the citizens of Riga. Additional land was donated by her son and more still by the city, after the ramparts were demolished. The gardens were planted with exotic flora from around the world, and a pavilion was constructed, which distributed mineral water to thirsty park-goers free of charge. Although high society soon claimed the park as its own, by the late 19th century, the area became the domain of commoners, especially local servants out to meet potential suitors. At the northwest entrance there is a monument to the founder of the park – it's surrounded by a rose gar-

den and flanked by two stone lions that are often abused by both children and pigeons.

Enter the park at the intersection of Barona and Elizabetes streets and walk in the direction of the outdoor amphitheatre, past the kiosks once used as fruit stands. On your right you'll notice a **black monument** that resembles a tombstone and bears the date 23 October 1812 in German. The Italian governor Paulucci, who was largely responsible for the creation of Riga's current design of parks and boulevards, requested that he never be immortalised for his deeds while acting as a public servant. The citizens of Riga circumvented his wishes by erecting a monument that doesn't even mention his name, only the date on which he arrived in Riga. The original stone is located in the Dome Cloister, among other lesser-known fragments of the city's history.

If you'd like to take a break, the tiny wooden building to the right is a favourite meeting place for locals. You can enjoy hundreds of different teas at **Apsara** (Tērbatas 2; tel: 721 24 36; open daily 9am–11pm), as well as spirits and delicious desserts. Relax at a table downstairs or opt for one of dozens of cosy pillows laid out over the floor in Eastern fashion upstairs.

Just ahead is a **fountain**, which is the centrepiece of the park. Cast in Berlin in 1869, the original was replaced by a bronze copy only a few decades ago. It depicts two cherubs playing at the top and nymphs and mythical sea creatures below. To the right is an open-air **amphitheatre** that hosts concerts and other events when the fickle Latvian climate allows. It is, how-

ever, a year-round favourite of Russian pensioners, who come here to chat, play chess or backgammon, feed the pigeons and reminisce. Unfortunately, the original amphitheatre, whose stage was shaped like a clamshell, was burned down on a number of occasions, so we are left with the current Soviet-style reincarnation.

Flower Market

Exit the park at the corner of Elizabetes and Tērbatas streets and turn left to visit the **flower market**. Latvians spend more of their disposable income on flowers than any other European nationality, which might be the reason why this market is open 24 hours a day, even on holidays. If you happen to visit Latvians at their home, or for that matter nearly any social setting, especially birthday or name-day par-

Top: park fountain
Above: chess games in Wöhrmann Park

ties, flowers are absolutely essential, but be sure to buy bouquets with an odd number of flowers only, as even-numbered ones are meant for funerals and unhappy occasions. The market runs the length of the block, and stall owners will be quick to offer to sell you anything from giant sunflowers to delicate orchids for incredibly reasonable prices.

Beyond the market on the left is what remains of the original mineral-water pavilion. Several additions have been constructed over the years and these now house restaurants, bars, clubs and casinos. Unfortunately, this is all a far cry from water pavilion's past grandeur.

Orthodox Cathedral

Cross Brīvības bulvāris and walk to the **Pareizticīgo Katedrāle** (Orthodox Cathedral). Built from 1876 to 1884, this massive monument to Russian-Byzantine architecture was meant to leave an impression on the tsar's Latvian subjects, who were mostly Lutheran or Catholic at the time. Alexander II created this beautiful house of worship as part of a centuries-old plan to 'russify' the empire's non-Slavic inhabitants. The message was clear to all that passed: these golden domes are examples of the power of Russia. Ironically, it was an important Russian communist who was offended by the building on her visit to Riga in the early 1960s – the minister of culture for the USSR ordered the golden crosses to be sawn off, and the premises were converted into a planetarium, a process that destroyed priceless frescoes inside. Nowadays, the building serves its original purpose as a church, but without the political agenda. Its six cupolas, including the one over the belfry, and its yellow-brick façade were completely renovated in 2005.

The Esplanade

Right behind the cathedral is the **Esplanāde** (Esplanade Park). An ancient hill called Kubes Kalns, whose caves were inhabited by hermits and the city's homeless, once stood here, but it was completely levelled in 1784 for fear that an invading army might capture it and use it to bombard the city. The sandy plain that remained was used as a parade ground for the military, until it was finally turned into a park; this was later used as the location for the 700th anniversary of Riga in 1901. During the Soviet occupation it was dedicated to fallen Bolsheviks from 1919.

At the far end of the park is a red granite statue of Latvia's most illustrious poet, playwright and political activist, **Rainis** (1865–1929).

Right: the flower market

As a socialist and participant in the 1905 Revolution, Rainis, born Jānis Pliekšāns, fled Latvia with his wife Aspazija, one of Latvia's greatest writers, and lived in exile in Switzerland; he lived here for the next 14 years, penning his most famous works. He returned to Latvia in 1920 and was later elected to the Latvian parliament. Ironically, his past as a socialist made him acceptable to the Soviet authorities, despite his overt Latvian patriotism. Today, both Latvian nationalists, a dwindling number of elderly communists and a new generation of Russian-speaking activists all use his statue as a rallying point.

National Art Museum

Ahead to the right is the imposing **Valsts mākslas muzejs** (National Art Museum; Valdemāra 10a; tel: 732 44 61; open Wed–Mon 11am–5pm; admission fee), an unusual building considering it was designed in the neo-Baroque style at the beginning of the 20th century, when Art Nouveau was in vogue. However, the interior is decorated in the latter fashion, especially the banisters of the marble staircases. Above on the ceiling are landscape murals by one of Latvia's old masters, Vilhelms Purvītis, who also served as curator of the museum. In addition to his paintings are works of art by the nation's best artists, including Rozentāls, Annus, Valters, Padegs and Liberts, whose work was mistakenly labelled as Russian art at a recent auction at Sotheby's in London.

To the left, at No. 13 Kalpaka, is one of the most impressive examples of early 20th-century architecture in Riga. The interior is rich in Art Nouveau embellishments, especially the stained-glass windows in the staircases, but the red brick exterior is neo-Gothic. Now home to the **Mākslas akadēmija** (Academy of Arts), it was built by the Riga Stock Exchange Committee, who chose the nostalgic style to honour Riga's mercantile past as a member of the Hanseatic League. Its elaborate, multicoloured façade and soaring spires recall medieval vistas.

Latvian National Theatre

Continue up Valdemāra until you reach **Latvijas Nacionālais teātris** (Latvian National Theatre) on your right side, at No. 2 Kronvalda bulvāris. The theatre is not only significant as an architectural monument and a venue for culture, but also as the

Above: self-portrait of Jānis Rozentāls
Left: sculpture fronting the National Art Museum

official birthplace of the Latvian nation. It was here in November of 1918 that a convention of Latvian intelligentsia proclaimed independence from the former Russian Empire and the revolutionary USSR. Completed in 1902, the former Second City Russian theatre was built in a combination of Baroque, classical and Renaissance styles. The entire building, including the interior, was completely renovated in 2003 and continues to draw sell-out crowds for performances of classic and modern Latvian plays and musicals.

Kronvalda Park

If you still have enough energy for a walk, you can take the picturesque tree-lined pathway to the right of the theatre that leads into **Kronvalda Park**. One of the city's most beautiful green spaces, it straddles the meandering Riga canal, which can be crossed along the way by footbridges. The path eventually ends at a small pagoda erected by the Chinese Embassy as a gift to the city. The pagoda has become a favourite retreat of young lovers searching for a place to kiss in relative privacy.

From here it's only a short distance to **Pētera-Pāvila baznīca** (Church of Sts Peter and Paul), in what's left of the **old citadel**. Walk up Miķela from Kronvalda bulvāris and turn left onto Citadeles, until you see the neglected spire of the sky-blue house of worship. Also known as the Ave Sol concert hall, it replaced a much older Lutheran church that was used by the Swedish garrison billeted here in the 17th century.
The ancient citadel and the original church were nearly completely destroyed when a Russian cannon-ball struck an ammunition depot, heralding the end of the siege of Riga as well as Scandinavian domination in the region. Constructed at the end of the 18th century, the church is adorned with unique Masonic symbols, including cherubs encircling a golden pyramid. A statue to a local Russian general's wife, Anna Kern, who had the distinction of being Alexander Pushkin's muse, is located in the courtyard.

Alternatively, follow Valdemāra from the theatre until you reach **Vanšu tilts**. Augusts Voss was a communist turncoat who, as leader of the Latvian Communist Party, was more interested in impressing the bosses in Moscow than helping his own people. However, in 1977 he ordered the construction of this modern bridge, which seems to be his only lasting contribution to society. Today, over 60,000 vehicles cross it daily, not including public buses. The left side of the bridge affords passers-by with excellent views of Old Riga and its many church spires.

Above: Chinese pagoda in Kronvalda Park

5. ART NOUVEAU DISTRICT (see map p49)

Explore the largest concentration of early 20th-century Art Nouveau buildings in Europe, including masterpieces by prolific Russian architect Mikhail Eisenstein.

Nearly a third of all buildings in the city centre are Art Nouveau in style, making Riga one of the largest open-air galleries of this flamboyant architectural fashion on the continent. By the time of its 700th anniversary in 1901, Riga was the third-largest port and fifth-largest city in the Russian Empire. Business was booming, and the antiquated laws prohibiting the construction of brick buildings outside the fortress had been repealed decades earlier. The city was poised for growth on an unprecedented scale, just as Art Nouveau was in vogue throughout Europe.

Known locally by its German name, Jugendstil, it was considered to be an optimistic search for beauty and individuality that began at the close of the 19th century. Many of the city's most expressive masterpieces were created in the years leading up to 1906, when a shift toward more subtle, geometric and conservative designs began to gain favour. This is largely blamed on international influences and the pessimism that followed the failure of the 1905 Revolution. The early works, however, such as the buildings on Alberta and Elizabetes, are renowned for the rich ornamentation of their façades, with curvy women, mythical creatures and a wealth of flora and fauna. Many of these are the brainchild of the prolific designer Mikhail Eisenstein (1867–1921), father of the illustrious Russian filmmaker and director of *Battle-*

Above: 10b Elizabetes Street

ship Potemkin, Sergei Eisenstein, who was born in Riga in 1898. Although you could take a stroll down any street in the city centre and view beautiful Art Nouveau buildings, the following tour will lead you past some of Riga's most spectacular and celebrated Jugendstil edifices.

Elizabetes Street

For a truly magnificent example of early Art Nouveau, begin at **No. 10b Elizabetes iela**. Easily recognised by its blue-brick façade, the building features sculptures of two improbably long human faces on either side of a peacock – one of the symbols of Art Nouveau. Erected in 1903, it is one of Eisenstein's crowning achievements and one of the city's most photographed sights. Today it houses luxury apartments and a beauty salon.

To the right, at **No. 10a Elizabetes**, is another one of Eisenstein's masterpieces, built the same year. Its façade is richly embellished with a variety of Art Nouveau motifs, but don't miss the relief of an anthropomorphised sun under the balcony and the unusually shaped windows on the top floor. The building across the street at **No. 33 Elizabetes** is yet another of Eisenstein's works, dating from 1901. One of his earliest major designs, it incorporates several different styles including Jugendstil and Eclecticism. The amazing detail on the façade includes larger-than-life sculptures of Atlas-like men supporting balconies on their shoulders.

Turn right here – at the junction – and proceed until you reach the stylised dragons guarding the entrance of **No. 8 Antonijas**. Designed in 1903 by one of Latvia's finest architects, Konstantīns Pēkšēns, it lacks the flamboyant ornamentation of Eisenstein's work, yet it exudes a classic understated elegance rarely seen in Art Nouveau structures of the period. It houses one of Riga's best Russian restaurants, **Traktieris** (Antonijas 8; tel: 733 24 55; open noon–11pm), which serves authentic Slavic food and drink served by waiters and waitresses in traditional costume.

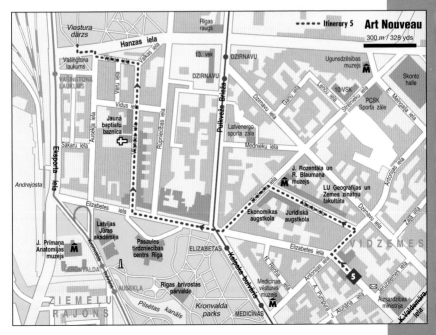

Alberta Street

To the left is the beginning of **Alberta iela**, Riga's most famous Art Nouveau street. Nearly every building on the block is a Jugendstil marvel, with most designed by Mikhail Eisenstein. Nos 2, 2a, 4, 6, 8 and 13 were all the brainchildren of the illustrious architect, not to mention a few around the corner on Strēlnieku. The first five are located next to one another on the right-hand side of the street. Sadly, some of the buildings are in a poor state of repair, largely due to the former Soviet belief in communal living. The seven-to ten-room apartments of the original owners were divided up among as many families after World War II, wreaking havoc on some of the city's most unique architectural treasures. Although some have been privatised since the regaining of Latvian independence, many are still home to unfortunate inhabitants who have to queue up every morning just to use the toilet or kitchen.

The buildings are works of art, and one could spend hours looking at their statues and reliefs. Nearly every space is filled with an element that conveys a symbolic meaning, typical of Art Nouveau's tenet of *horror vacui* or 'fear of a vacuum'. Although seemingly similar when viewed one next to another, the apartment buildings were intended to be completely different. Don't miss the sphinxes, screaming gargoyles and the windows shaped like keyholes. Philosophy students will no doubt be interested to know that liberal thinker Sir Isaiah Berlin (1909–1997) was born in Riga and lived in **No. 2a** from 1909–15.

Latvian architect Eižens Laube designed the building on the left-hand side of the street, at **No. 11**, in 1908. Unlike many of the other Jugendstil façades on Alberta, Laube's is an example of national romanticism, popular with architects of the later period, who strived to create a style typical of their region. It lacks ornate decoration, but is unique in its design nonetheless.

At the end of Alberta on the right, at **No. 12**, is an impressive structure that also houses the **Jana Rozentāla un Rūdolfa Blaumana muzejs** (Museum of Jānis Rozentāls and Rūdolfs Blaumanis; Alberta 12; tel: 733 16 41; open

Wed–Sun 11am–6pm; admission fee). It successfully combines both Renaissance and medieval design with Art Nouveau, and was a showcase for architect Konstantīns Pēkšēns, who owned the building and had his offices on the ground floor. His colleagues Eižens Laube and Aleksandrs Vanags also lived in the building, as did the artist Jānis Rozentāls and the writer Rūdolfs Blaumanis. The museum, dedicated to the latter two men, includes period furniture and paintings by Rozentāls, who may have also designed the apartment. Even if you don't want to walk up the steps to the top-floor museum, it's worth a quick look at one of the finest decorative staircases in the city. The foyer frescoes were restored in 2005.

The building at **No. 13 Alberta** is the perfect bookend to the street. The most ornately embellished of its neighbours, it was designed by Eisenstein and completed in 1904. It is an ideal illustration of the previously mentioned principle of fear of empty space, and each of its Art Nouveau maidens and mythical creatures seems to have a personality of its own. Ironically, this most artistically expressive of Eisenstein's creations, and perhaps the most symbolic of Art Nouveau's optimism and belief in beauty, was used as a secret military institution by the Soviets. It has been completely renovated and now provides office space for embassies, NGOs and the Riga Graduate School of Law.

Strēlnieku Street

Turn left on Strēlnieku and you'll be rewarded with a view of yet another one of Eisenstein's creations – at **No. 4a**. Built in 1905, it is now home to the Riga School of Economics. Although it has been completely renovated, many of its interior decorations were destroyed during the Soviet era, when the building was used as a youth hostel. On the corner of the intersection, at **No. 2**, is a typical example of what is often referred to as perpendicular Art Nouveau, where vertical elements on the façades of buildings are overstated to achieve a decorative effect.

Left: Art Nouveau staircase at 13 Alberta Street
Above: detail, 2a Alberta Street

You've just seen many of Riga's most spectacular architectural wonders, but there are many more to explore if you wish to continue. If not, you can have lunch at **Ai Karamba!** (Pulkveža Brieža 2; tel: 733 46 72; open 8am–midnight, Fri–Sat 8am–1am, Sun 10am–midnight) around the corner. Housed in a beautiful, eclectic-style brick building from the late 19th century, it's the nearest thing to a classic American diner that Riga has to offer and serves the best breakfast in the city from morning till night.

Towards Vīlandes Street

From here, head west down Elizabetes in the direction of the river. Nearly every building on the right side of the street is an architectural treasure, but we'll turn our attention to a conspicuous slab of concrete on the opposite side in front of the Riga World Trade Centre. A gift from the director of the Checkpoint Charlie Museum in Germany, it is an original **fragment of the**

Berlin Wall and holds special significance for Latvians, who were also trapped behind the Iron Curtain.

The building with the magnificent tower built in 1898 at **No. 1 Vīlandes** was one of the last eclectic buildings to be constructed in Riga, displaying both Rococo and Baroque elements, but its interior is in the Art Nouveau style. It offers a unique glimpse of architecture in transition, from the old eclectic style that sought inspiration in the past, also called historicism, to Jugendstil. **No. 4** was erected ten years later and already reflects the subtler style of late Art Nouveau. The relief of a woman's face with her eyes closed signifies secrecy – a popular theme of the period.

A contemporary building at **No. 10** features a combination of styles, including an ornate Art Nouveau entrance, German Renaissance accents and a relief – depicting satyrs dancing with bare-breasted women – reminiscent of a Minoan fresco. The imposing edifice at **No. 11 Vīlandes** is yet another example of both eclectic and Art Nouveau elements sharing a common space. Built in 1899, it is one of Riga's first Jugendstil buildings.

Latvian Song and Dance Festival

From here it's only a short walk to **Viestura dārzs**, Riga's oldest public park and the site of the first Latvian Song and Dance Festival in 1873. A monument beside a shallow pool displays the faces of some of the festival's most illustrious participants and organisers. The park was created in 1721 by order of Peter the Great, who planted a tree here. The tree no longer exists, but a small plaque on a stone on the Hanzas iela side of the park marks the spot where it once grew. The colossal entrance gate was built in 1815 to celebrate Russia's victory over Napoleon's troops in 1812. A young J.F. Kennedy once stayed at Ausekļa 22, just east of the gate, during a student summer tour of Europe in 1939. Of the local populace he is said to have remarked, 'Latvians will always reach upwards.'

Above: No. 1 Vīlandes

6. MOSCOW DISTRICT *(see map p55)*

Rarely visited by tourists, the Moscow District (Maskavas Forštate, meaning 'Little Moscow') offers unique wooden architecture, impressive churches, the remnants of Jewish life in Riga as well as one of the largest marketplaces in Europe.

For hundreds of years this aptly named area of Riga has been home to a large population of Russians – from the 17th-century Old Believers escaping religious persecution in their homeland to the thousands of immigrants who arrived during the years of Soviet occupation in search of a better life. All but ignored by tourists and often neglected by its own people, this historic neighbourhood of cobbled streets, dilapidated wooden buildings and ageing Art Nouveau façades is among the least affluent of the Latvian capital's districts, but is worthy of a brief tour nonetheless.

Indeed, the area's unique wooden architecture that was once a blessing has now become its curse. Many of the rotting 19th-century buildings are protected by the state, and consequently cannot be demolished to make room for new construction. Unfortunately, the cost of renovating these 100-year-old homes and offices is often astronomical, an economic pitfall for potential investors. This catch-22 situation meant to preserve the Moscow District's historic atmosphere for posterity could also sound its death knell. Further down the road, on Krasta iela, where empty lots once stood, you'll find the exact opposite. The fruits of the Latvian economic boom are clearly visible here in the form of strip malls and a seemingly endless procession of foreign car dealerships built on land that was unencumbered by the ghosts of the past.

Above: Central Market
Right: detail of a door in the Moscow District

Central Market

The most obvious and notable of the district's sights is the huge complex of the **Centrāltir-gus** (Central Market; Prāgas 1; open daily 8am–5pm). Five 35-m (29-ft) high zeppelin hangars, built by the Germans in Vainode, south-western Latvia during World War I, were brought here in the 1920s. When refurbishment work to transform them into retail pavilions was completed in 1930, they formed one of the largest markets on the continent, covering more than 15,000 square metres (160,500 sq ft). It was also an exceptionally modern market, with an elaborate system of tunnels that connected refrigerated subterranean warehouses which were accessible by lifts.

The pavilions still serve their original function, each housing retail space for either meat, vegetables, fish, dairy or cereals. Beyond the pavilions you'll find hundreds of stalls selling anything from fresh fruits and berries to leather jackets and suspiciously inexpensive DVDs. Merchants often don't take kindly to being photographed and might even ask for a gratuity for posing for you. Ask for a sample of what they're selling and they'll usually brighten up, however. Unique finds at the market include *gotiņas* (little cows) cream sweets, delicious dill pickles in giant glass jars and the elusive hemp butter, a former Latvian staple, that has now become a rare delicacy.

Located behind the market are the so-called **Sarkanie spīķeri** (Red Warehouses), built decades before the market was even conceived. Constructed of red brick, the most typical examples can be seen at **Nos 1 and 8 Spīķeru iela**, and to the right, on Maskavas iela. Although some still

serve their intended purpose, many have been converted into retail space.

Academy of Sciences

Proceed down Prāgas until you reach one of the most lasting symbols of the old communist regime – the **Zinātnu akadēmija** (Academy of Sciences; Akadēmijas 1). Typical of the times, it was built ostensibly as the House of Collective Farms, even though no-one knew exactly what that meant or what its function might be. Like similar-style buildings constructed in the eastern bloc in the 1950s, it was dedicated to Stalin and was supposed to symbolise the power of the Soviet state. In classic Soviet fashion, a unique early 19th-century wooden structure, known as the Russian Bazaar, was torn down to implement

Above: trader at Central Market
Left: Academy of Sciences

the project. If you look closely you can see several hammers and sickles on the façade of the 'poor man's Empire State Building'.

To the left, at No. 7 Gogoļa, is the yellow, green and blue **Marijas pasludināšanas baznīca** (Orthodox Church of Virgin Mary Annunciation). The brightly coloured wooden structure was built in 1818 and features elaborate icons in an otherwise simply decorated interior.

From here continue along Gogoļa to the **ruins of the Big Choral Synagogue** or Die Greise Hor Shul, as it was once known in Yiddish, at the junction with Dzirnavu. On 4 July 1941 the Nazis herded hundreds of Jewish refugees, mostly from Lithuania, who had fled to the north ahead of the advancing German army, into the building. The synagogue was torched, and everyone perished. Today, the sparse ruins adorned with a menorah and a rock engraved with the year of the atrocity are a powerful reminder of the Holocaust in Latvia.

Church of Jesus

Head back down Gogoļa and turn left into Jēzusbaznīcas, towards the octagonal **Jēzus baznīca** (Church of Jesus; Elijas 18). The original house of worship was constructed in 1638, but barely survived two decades before it was razed by the retreating armies of Tsar Alexis Mikhailovich, who had unsuccessfully attacked Riga, then part of the Swedish Empire. Due to a series of disasters and a general period of hardship the church was only rebuilt in 1688, but it was not blessed with longevity. The troops of a different tsar, Peter the Great, burned the church down to the ground in 1710. Another church was built to replace it, but that too was torched, this time by the order of Riga itself in preparation for an assault by the armies of Napoleon. The French troops, however, never arrived, and the officer responsible for the mistake later committed suicide in disgrace. The current building dates back to the early 1820s, and its 37-m (121-ft) high steeple makes it the tallest wooden structure in Latvia. Its unique shape makes for an interesting interior, which is flanked by soaring white ionic columns.

If you've worked up a hunger, proceed down Jēzusbaznīcas in the direction of the river to Maskavas and catch an eastbound tram (No. 7 or 9) to the 'Lido atpūtas centrs' stop. Take a five- to 10-minute walk south until you reach the giant windmill of the **Lido Recreation Centre**, a massive log cabin on three floors that serves up authentic, inexpensive Latvian food, beer and music. It is also an amusement park with various attractions for kids. If you take the tram in the opposite direction within a few stops you'll arrive at the National Opera at the edge of Old Riga.

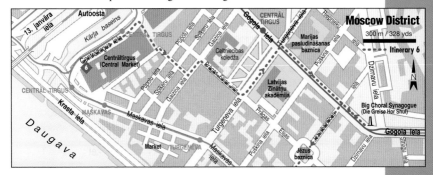

7. PĀRDAUGAVA (THE LEFT BANK) *(see map p57)*

Beautiful parks, a bustling market and Soviet megalomaniac monuments are just a short walk or tram ride away from Old Riga.

Unlike other Riga suburbs, Pārdaugava's shallow shores were largely ignored for centuries, until a freak occurrence changed their destiny. In the late 17th century the River Daugava inexplicably changed its course, leaving a deeper channel on the left side than the right, by present-day Old Riga. The city's commercial prosperity was at risk, and a series of far-reaching projects to shore up both banks of the river was undertaken. Still, it wasn't until the end of the 18th century that the area gained in economic importance. A road linking St Petersburg, capital of the Russian Empire, to Europe via Riga was finally completed, and the mostly Latvian inhabitants of Pārdaugava – many of them escaped serfs working as ferrymen, river pilots, stevedores and porters – were suddenly in demand. The seasonal pontoon bridge spanning the river in the summer months buzzed with traffic and activity.

Regular ferry, train and tram services via two new steel bridges were established in the 19th century, making the once-difficult passage to the Left Bank child's play. Summer cottages and lavish mansions were constructed as well as countless warehouses and factories. Even today, Pārdaugava's character is decidedly Latvian, and nearly 25 percent of the city's population lives here. Unlike the crowded old town or geometrically sound centre, the Left Bank is a potpourri of overgrown parkland, meandering, almost illogically laid streets, sprawling industrial zones and suburban houses, whose high fences hide a wealth of private gardens and miniature apple and pear orchards.

The following is a walking tour of some of Pārdaugava's best sights and is meant for people who don't mind a leisurely stroll that could take up to two

Above: Arcadia Park

hours in one direction. However, should you require transportation, you can board tram route No. 10 from the Old Riga side of the river and stop at any of the sights along the way.

Latvian Railway Museum

Walk across Akmens tilts (literally, the Stone Bridge), which replaced the ancient pontoon bridge that also served as a dock for incoming ships. It was only open during sunlight hours and was removed each autumn before the water began to freeze. The current 20th-century structure decorated with enormous lamps may not be as aesthetically pleasing as the former, but it is certainly more practical. From here pedestrians are afforded excellent views of the steel train bridge, television tower and Central Market to the left, the modern Vanšu Bridge and Hansabanka skyscraper to the right, Old Riga behind and the golden stars of the Victory monument ahead – not to mention the wide expanse of the river.

Continue walking straight on until you reach the red brick building of **Latvijas dzelzceļa muzejs** (Latvian Railway Museum; Uzvaras 2–4; tel: 723 28 49; open Tues–Sat 10am–5pm; admission fee; www.railwaymuseum.lv), which was once used as a repair station for trains. Inside are various exhibits, including old tools, uniforms and even a few old railway carriages. Don't miss the locomotives on display behind the museum, including one that saw action during World War II and another that was one of only 10 experimental locomotives built in the entire Soviet Union, typically named the Vladimir Lenin. The museum is also a popular venue for rock concerts at weekends.

Victory Park

Proceed down Uzvaras in the direction of the megalomaniac monstrosity that is **Uzvaras piemineklis** (Victory Monument). Built in 1985, the ensemble of copper statues depicting the motherland and gun-toting Red Army soldiers, as well as a 79-m (260-ft) tall obelisk crowned by five stars, each representing a year of World War II, is extremely controversial. Although the sacrifices of Soviet troops in defeating Nazism is certainly worthy of commemoration, the so-called liberation of Latvia was a brutal occupation during which countless tens upon thousands of people were raped, tortured, executed or deported to forced labour camps in Siberia to die of exposure, starvation or exhaustion.

The idea of giving the local populace a more communist-friendly object of veneration than the Latvian Freedom Monument was only

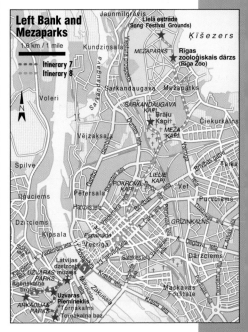

accepted by the Russian inhabitants of Riga, who to this day lay flowers here on their wedding days. It is also the rallying point for red-flag wavers and war veterans, who often celebrate World War II victories here by singing Stalin-era songs and drinking copious amounts of vodka. Two Latvian nationalists even tried to 'liberate' the city of its presence with a homemade bomb in the late 1990s. The monument suffered little damage but the would-be patriots both perished.

Uzvaras parks (Victory Park), which surrounds the structure, is Riga's largest park. Curiously, it wasn't a Latvian, Russian or German who was responsible for its creation, but rather an Englishman – George Armitsted, Riga's mayor from 1901 to 1912. He actively campaigned to destroy the useless fortifications here that had somehow managed to escape the wrecking ball. Eventually, the old Kobronskanst fort originating from Swedish rule in the 17th century was levelled, and a lush park named in honour of Peter the Great was born. It was renamed Uzvaras parks during the first Latvian republic in the 1920s.

If you'd like to explore the park further or perhaps visit the **Āgenskalna tirgus** (Āgenskalns market; Nometņu 64; tel: 761 15 49; open Mon–Sat 7.30am–8pm, Sun 7.30–7pm), then head down Bāriņu to the right. Although nowhere near as large as the Central Market, this one has a quaint neighbourhood atmosphere, with every shopper seeming to be on first-name terms with the stall owners. The red-brick pavilion was designed by the renowned Riga architect Reinhold Schmaeling in 1911.

Arcadia Park

From the Victory Monument, proceed left on the tree-lined Uzvaras bulvāris until you reach **Arkādijas parks** (Arcadia Park). The area between the railway and F. Brīvzemnieka and O. Vācieša streets was once a private estate, which was later sold to the Waldschloeschen Brewery that would later become Aldaris. At the close of the 19th century the land was appropriated by the city, and Riga's prolific landscape architect Georg Kuphaldt drew up plans for a grand park. The innovative designer decided to divert the River Mārupīte to flow through the park and even created an artificial waterfall. A restaurant and bandstand were also constructed, but much of the park's former glory has faded over the years due to neglect. Today, the calm waters of the meandering stream are the park's greatest asset.

Above and right: statues, Victory Park

Although by no means an essential sight, the **Ojāra Vācieša memoriālais muzejs** (Ojārs Vācietis Memorial Museum; Ojāra Vācieša 19; tel: 761 87 75; open daily 1–7pm, Thur, Sat, Sun 11am–5pm; admission fee) is worth a quick peek if you have the time and inclination towards literature and wooden architecture. The illustrious Latvian poet Ojārs Vācietis (1933–83) lived and worked in this 200-year-old building from 1960 until the day of his death. Some of his personal possessions, including a pair of boxing gloves, are on display, as well as a collection of his works. A small café and gift shop are also here.

Gulag Memorial

Follow F. Brīvzemnieka, which winds around the park, to the bridge at the top of the hill. From here you can see the railway network that leads into the city centre and the black spire of Dome Cathedral across the river. Take the stairs at the far end of the bridge to the **Tornakalns station**, where you'll find two **monuments** dedicated to the unfortunate citizens deported to the gulag.

Beside the train tracks is a cattle car marked with Cyrillic letters and hammers and sickles that was used by the Soviets to send tens of thousands of Latvian citizens to a horrible end in Siberia. On the night of 13–14 June 1941 nearly 16,000 people, among them 3,000 children, were woken up at gunpoint and told to pack warm clothes for a long trip. Many were never heard from again. More mass deportations followed, the largest of which took place in March 1949, when 42,000 people disappeared in a single night. With little food, water and a lack of proper sanitation, many of the young, elderly and infirm didn't survive the arduous journey. When one considers that the population of the nation at the time was roughly 2 million, the numbers are staggering. The second and, in truth, less impressive memorial is 200m (650 ft) behind the station to the right. It is comprised of several granite stones symbolising the deported.

Indriķa Street

From here you can take an eastbound train back to the centre or simply board tram No. 10 from the bridge for a ride back to Old Riga. If you'd like to explore a little more, head down the cobblestoned Indriķa iela in the opposite direction to the station. On the left is an excellent example of a wooden Art Nouveau building complete with a large tower topped with a weathervane. Just ahead on the left at Nos 3–5 Torņakalna is **Tornakalna baznīca**, also known as Luther's Church, built in 1888. Perched on top of the hill, its yellow-and-

Above: deportation sculpture, Torņakalns station

red-brick neo-Gothic façade is an impressive sight. The interior is typically austere, apart from the elaborate wooden ceiling and stained-glass windows.

Further ahead to the right is a rare Art Nouveau bridge, made more original by the fact that it is constructed of concrete, a technological innovation regarded with suspicion at the time. To the left, at **No. 8 Indriķa**, is a tiny red house built after the fire of 1812. Although the building is not particularly remarkable on its own, it has an interesting history. It was built in the city centre but then donated to the church to prevent its destruction at the hands of eager developers. It was completely dismantled and then reassembled in its current location.

8. Mežaparks   *(see map p57)*

Europe's first garden city has regained its prestigious reputation since independence, and many of its Art Nouveau cottages have been restored to their former glory. Relax by the lake, visit the zoo or take a look at the enormous Song and Dance Festival grounds.

Mežaparks, once known as Kaiserwald, has the distinction of being Europe's first garden city. While in other cities on the continent the idea of creating the antique version of a gated community was being contemplated, Riga's city council had already approved plans for the founding of a natural suburb, where only summer cottages could be built on large plots of land to ensure a healthy lifestyle for their inhabitants. The elite of the city were suffocating in the squalor of the old town, which lacked proper sanitation and was heavily polluted, and jumped at the chance to buy property on the shore of Lake Ķīšezers, only 4km (2½ miles) from the city centre.

By 1901 the main road to Mežaparks had already been constructed, and beautiful villas that resembled Swiss chalets embellished with Art Nouveau decoration were erected at breakneck speed. Even the streets that traverse the hilly pine forest were designed to mimic natural pathways, hence the complete lack of straight lines.

Although the area was initially the exclusive domain of wealthy Germans, well-to-do Latvian merchants and professionals eventually became homeowners in Mežaparks. On the eve of World War II, Baltic Germans were compelled to 'return' to the fatherland, leaving vacant hundreds of homes that would soon be coveted by invaders from the east. Initially, it was the upper echelon of the Soviet occupation forces that moved into the sumptuous homes, but after the war the villas of the bourgeoisie would each house several immigrant families – to the detriment of the buildings and the neighbourhood in general. For much of the Soviet era, Mežaparks would be regarded as a slum. Today, many of

Above: attractions in Mežaparks include watersports

the buildings have been returned to their original owners and their relatives, and the area has regained its original status as a place where the rich and famous dwell.

City Cemeteries

Mežaparks is a short ride from K. Barona in the city centre on tram route No. 11, but there are also some noteworthy cemeteries on the way should you wish to pay them a visit. The first is **Pokrova kapi**. Exit the tram at the Mēness iela stop and walk straight ahead, turning right onto Senču. Ahead, on the right-hand side, you'll see the cemetery and a small Orthodox chapel with a detached belfry in the distance. Just beyond are the headstones of tsarist-era bureaucrats and their epitaphs in old Cyrillic script, telling of their good deeds on earth. To the left, by the street, is the final resting place of fallen Red Army soldiers, easily recognised by a relief of a golden soldier bearing the flag of the USSR. A small, bizarre memorial also tells the tale, in Russian, of nearly a dozen local orphans who were supposedly drained of their blood by the Nazis. Although armies throughout the 20th century have been known to force non-combattants to supply blood for injured soldiers, it's difficult to know for certain if this actually happened or if it is yet another product of Soviet propaganda. The cemetery is rarely visited, with the exception of a few Latvians out walking their dogs.

Across the street is **Lielie kapi** (Great Cemetery). It was established in 1773 after Catherine II banned the interring of the deceased in churches. Many of Riga's most renowned writers, professionals and statesmen of various nationalities are buried here, including city architect Reinhold Schmaeling, illustrious collector of folk songs Krišjānis Barons and cultural and political activist Krišjānis Valdemārs. Unfortunately, many of the beautiful headstones 'disappeared' after World War II,

Above: windmill in Mežaparks
Right: sculpture at the entrance to Mežaparks

somehow finding their way to Russian family plots across the Soviet Union with new epitaphs. The place now feels like more of a park than a cemetery, its centuries-old family crypts an ambient backdrop for joggers and skaters.

Return to Miera iela and continue on tram route No. 11 from Kazarmu for two stops until you reach **Brāļu kapi** (Brothers' Cemetery). Second only to the Freedom Monument in the hearts of Latvians, the final resting place of the nation's freedom fighters was completed in 1936. Walk down Aizsaules iela past dozens of flower stalls until you reach the gates inscribed with the years 1915–20. Follow the long travertine footpath to the steps that lead to the eternal flame. From here, the main complex of the cemetery can be seen, including hundreds of symmetrically ordered white headstones, giant sculptures

and reliefs of ancient warriors, and the centrepiece of the ensemble – Mother Latvia. To the right is **Meža kapi**, a working cemetery, where former presidents and statesmen are buried among the ranks of average citizens, both Latvian and Russian.

Historic Homes

Return to the tram stop and continue your journey to Mežaparks, disembarking five stops later at Hamburgas iela. Although one could wander the area for hours, this short tour will point out some of its most historic homes. On the corner at **No. 1 Sudrabu Edžus** is one of the first villas to be constructed in Mežaparks. The kitchen and servants' quarters were housed on the ground floor, while the owners occupied the first floor.

Walk down Hamburgas until you reach **No. 9**, built in 1908. Formerly known as Villa Adele, it has a beautiful façade that belies an ugly history, when the building served as a hotel and fun palace for visiting Soviet generals. An imposing fence patrolled by a large force of armed men once surrounded the building. Today it is the residence of the German ambassador. A collage of modern renovations and overgrown decay, the street perfectly illustrates the gulf between the haves and have-nots in Latvia. Take for instance the example of the pristine yellow home at No. 6, as compared with the ivy-covered wooden building at No. 21 that looks on the verge of collapse. **No. 23**, built in 1909 and complete with a cross on its façade, is the residence of the Swiss ambassador. Built in 1910, **No. 25**, with its expertly manicured gardens is perhaps the most impressive building on the street.

At this point, turn left, then take another left into Lībekas iela. Designed by a Baltic German, many of Mežaparks' meandering streets – Stokholmas (Stockholm), Lībekas (Luebeck), Visbijas (Visby), Gdaņskas (Danzig) – are a tribute to Riga's Hanseatic sister cities. Turn right into Pēterupes and proceed to

Above: folk groups celebrating the harvest in Mežaparks. **Right:** local wicker crafts

Kokneses prospekts. From here you can either take the tram to the next stop or walk the short distance to the zoo. Across the street is the **Gustavs Ādolfs café** (Kokneses prospekts 13a; tel: 751 86 79; open 11am–11pm), which offers Latvian food and drink as well as a pleasant summer terrace.

Riga Zoo and Song Festival Grounds

Rīgas Nacionālais zooloģiskais dārzs (Riga Zoo; Meža prospekts 1; tel: 751 84 09; open daily April–September 10am–6pm, October–March 10am–4pm; admission fee) has been in operation since 1912. It is home to over 3,000 animals, not including invertebrates, and its location on 16 hectares (2½ acres) of land on the southwestern shore of Lake Ķīšezers is sublime. Among its best exhibits is the tropical house that provides hand-dryers for your glasses in case they fog up. Inside are alligators, crocodiles, snakes and a staggering number of insects. However, if noble beasts are more to your liking, you can also observe lions, tigers, bears, wolves and a host of exotic fauna from around the globe. A hilltop café is also available with great views of the lake below. Be prepared to spend at least an hour or two at the zoo.

To the left of the zoo is the main entrance to the park. In the summer a carnival atmosphere pervades the place, and a number of stalls sell food and refreshments, while others rent bicycles and in-line skates. The park also provides various attractions such as merry-go-rounds and even a small roller-coaster of sorts. Proceed down the paved footpath until you reach Pāvu iela. If you'd like to explore the **lake shore** and perhaps rent paddle boats or even a jet ski, then turn right here and take the shady path to the lake. It's also a great place for a picnic or sunbathing.

If you proceed down the main footpath you'll eventually reach a fork in the road. Take a left to reach the **Lielā estrāde** (Song Festival Grounds). It is here that roughly every five years the Latvian Song Festival is held. The ample stage can accommodate 20,000 singers and the surrounding benches and grassy spaces can seat tens of thousands more spectators. It also hosts large concerts by international pop and rock stars.

Above: Riga Zoo

excursions

Excursions

1. JŪRMALA   *(see map p68)*

Riga's summer playground offers over 20km (12½ miles) of white-sand beaches, dozens of luxury spas and excellent alfresco dining.

Trains leave Riga station nearly every 20 minutes during the summer and roughly every hour in low season. The journey to the main town of Majori should take no longer than 40 minutes.

Although the nobility of the Duchy of Courland had known about the pristine beaches and natural springs of the area for many years, it wasn't until the 19th century that the narrow spit of land sandwiched between the sea and the River Lielupe, and known as Jūrmala, became a popular destination for the inhabitants of Riga. Its close proximity to the city and the introduction of a railway line in 1877 made day trips to Jūrmala convenient and affordable. Summer cottages were built at breakneck speed, but World War I put an end to all development until the 1920s, when artists, intellectuals and politicians descended on the loose federation of little towns on the Baltic.

During the Soviet era, Jūrmala became one of the best-loved destinations for holidaymakers from the USSR, but a larger number of tourists also heralded the creation of megalithic Soviet-style concrete hotels and unchecked urban sprawl. Thankfully, many of these ageing dinosaurs have been completely renovated. Despite the modernisation of the area, however, a nostalgia for the communist heyday seems to linger in many of the hearts and minds of its inhabitants, many of whom are Russian-speakers who retired here before independence.

Majori

The lovely town of **Majori** has the most to offer in terms of tourist infrastructure. At the train station cross the street and walk one block until you reach **Jomas iela**, a pedestrian street lined with shops, cafés and restaurants. All the streets on the left-hand side lead to the beach. If you walk until the end of Jomas, you can visit **Seno spēkratu izstāde** (Antique Car Exhibit; Turaidas 11; tel: 926 33 29; open May 1–September 30 11am–6pm; free), which has dozens of antique cars on display as well as some rather ancient-looking motorcycles. The museum also displays an automobile from 1907 that once belonged to Tsar Nikolai II.

Walk down Turaidas iela in the direction of the sea and make a left on Jūras iela (Sea Street). Nearly every building on the street is an architectural gem from the early 20th century, and many are excellent examples of wooden Art Nouveau. If you take another left on Pliekšāna iela you'll pass **Raina un Aspazijas vasarnīca** (Summer Cottage of Rainis and Aspazija; Pliekšāna 5–7;

Left: sandcastles in Jūrmala
Right: historic beachfront building, Majori

tel: 776 44 95; open Wed–Sun 11am–6pm; admission fee), where two of Latvia's most celebrated writers once spent their summer holidays. Among the personal affects of the authors is a collection of 7,000 books in 11 languages.

Dubultu luterānu baznīca (Dubulti Lutheran Church; Baznīcas 13) is the most impressive house of worship in the area, and its soaring spire can be seen from a great distance. Built in 1909, it is, astonishingly, one of the only Art Nouveau churches ever constructed in Latvia. Take the train one stop further to Dubulti or walk down Z. Meierovica prospekts for about 30 minutes.

2. SIGULDA   *(see map p68)*

With no fewer than three castles, a network of clearly marked hiking trails and the scenic Gauja River Valley, Sigulda has something for everyone.

Trains and buses leave Riga for Sigulda roughly every hour. The journey usually takes about 60 minutes.

Often referred to as the Switzerland of Latvia, Sigulda's picturesque rolling hills and valleys are among the nation's most scenic, and its medieval castle ruins make it one of the country's most visited destinations. It was settled by Liv tribesmen as early as the 11th century, but their luck ran out when German crusaders conquered the area, replacing the Chieftain Kaupo's wooden fortress with the stone castle of Siegewald in 1207. A town sprouted up at the foot of the castle, and soon other strongholds were built, as well as a church, and the community began to thrive.

Prosperity came to an abrupt end with the Great Livonian War (1558–82), when Russian troops attacked the town and its fortifications over a period of decades. Shortly after peace was declared, another war broke out, this time between Poland and Sweden, placing Sigulda directly in harm's way. The original castle was destroyed, and the town became an all-but-forgotten backwater, until the Riga–Pskov railway revived its economy in the 19th century. With the pretty town accessible, tourists began to visit it, enjoying its beautiful vistas and romantic castle ruins. Today, Sigulda draws hundreds of thousands of visitors and has a well-oiled tourism infrastructure.

Turaida Highlights

The town's most remarkable landmark is the **Turaidas muzejrezervāts** (Turaida Museum Reserve; Turaidas 10; tel: 797 14 02; open daily 10am–6pm; admission fee), which has a wide variety of sights spread out over several acres of land. Originally built in 1214, the reconstructed red-brick **Turaida Castle** is perched high above the valley and offers excellent views from its guard tower, as well as a small museum dedicated to the Liv tribes that once inhabited the surrounding hills. You can also buy Latvian jewellery, based on ancient Baltic artefacts unearthed in the area. Just outside the castle grounds is one of Latvia's oldest wooden churches, dating to 1750.

Not far from the church, under a giant linden tree, you'll find the grave of Maija (1601–20), **Turaidas Roze** (Rose of Turaida), a young Latvian maiden who was killed after refusing to submit to a lech-erous Polish soldier. Legend has it that she was in love with a young commoner, but the Pole asked for her hand in marriage, which she refused. Mad with jealousy and lust, he devised a plan to lure her to a nearby cave where he might have his way with her. Discovering his treach-ery too late, she presented him with a 'magic' scarf that could protect him from harm and to demonstrate its prop-erties she wore it around her neck and asked him to strike her with his sword. The foolish soldier lopped her head off, and now local newlyweds lay flowers here on their wedding day as a tribute to everlasting love.

Beyond the grave is **Dainu kalns** (Folksong Hill), a sculpture garden with excellent views of the castle and the surrounding valley. A hiking trail leads down to Gūtmaṇa ala (Gutmanis Cave) at the bottom of the hill, where it is believed that the Turaida Rose met her end. At nearly 19m (62ft) deep, 12m (40ft) wide and 10m (33ft) high, it is the largest cave in the Baltics. Its soft sandstone walls still bear inscriptions from as early as the 17th century.

Left: Turaida Castle. **Above:** Sigulda landscape
Right: sculpture in the grounds of Turaida Castle

Sigulda Castle

The remains of Sigulda's first castle are located just outside the centre of town. **Siguldas pils drupas** (Sigulda Castle ruins) look just as they did centuries earlier and have been largely untouched, allowing them to retain their original charm. The impressive stone tower is the best-preserved section of the castle, along with the shell of the former chapel with its long Gothic windows. The ruins now serve as an open-air concert hall in the summer.

Just across the way is the new **Siguldas pils** (Sigulda Castle), which is actually a 19th-century manor house currently housing an elegant restaurant, not to mention the city council. Thrill seekers can venture back to the city centre to **Siguldas bobslejtrase** (Sigulda Bobsleigh Track; Šveices 13; tel: 797 38 13; open Sat–Sun noon–5pm; admission fee), where experienced athletes will take you down the course, at speeds of over 100 km/h (60 mph).

3. BAUSKA REGION *(see map below)*

The city of Bauska is home to what are arguably the most impressive castle ruins in Latvia, and the nearby palaces at Rundāle and Mežotne are on a par with the finest Europe has to offer.

Buses leave Riga nearly every half hour. The journey should take about an hour and a half.

Built in 1433, **Bauskas pils** (Bauska Castle; Pilskalns; tel: 392 37 93; open daily 9am–6pm; admission fee), with its five guard towers and 4-m (13-ft) thick walls, was the last fortress to be constructed by the Livonian Order. The warrior monks were beginning to lose their powerful grip on Latvia and built the castle at the confluence of the Lielupe and Mūsa rivers to protect the land from incursions by Poles and Lithuanians. After the disintegration of the order, the

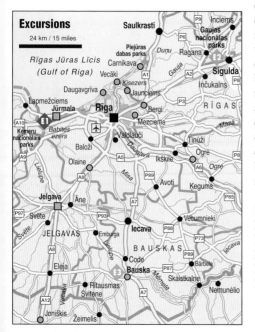

castle became the property of the dukes of Courland, who added a large residence to the medieval fortress which is currently undergoing renovations. It was blown up in 1706 by a retreating Russian army during the Great Northern War (1700–21) and abandoned thereafter. You can explore the ruins and climb to the observation deck in the tower for excellent views of the city and neighbouring countryside. There's also a small castle museum.

Rundāle Palace

Less than 10km (6 miles) west of Bauska is the most celebrated Baroque monument in the country, **Rundāles pils** (Rundāle Palace; tel: 396 22 74; open June–Aug 10am–

7pm, Sept–May 10am–5pm; admission fee; www.rpm.apollo.lv). The brainchild of Francesco Bartolomeo Rastrelli (1700–71), the renowned architect who would later build the Winter Palace in St Petersburg, the palace was commissioned by Duke Ernst Johan von Biron of Courland as a summer residence for his family; much of the exterior of the building was completed between 1736 and 1740. The duke, however, was granted his title by Tsarina Anna (1693–1740) and soon fell out of favour after her death. He was arrested and exiled to a backwater of Russia, until Catherine the Great restored his standing in 1765, when work resumed on the palace. The Baroque and Rococo masterpiece was finally finished three years later and passed from one noble family to the next until it became the property of the new Latvian Republic in 1920.

Less than a third of its 138 rooms have been restored to their original glory, but a tour of the duke's resplendent presentation halls and private apartments are enough to make your jaw drop. The duchess's bedroom has also recently been renovated, and the painstaking task of restoring the minute details of other historic rooms is currently underway. Visitors can also see two separate exhibitions, one displaying some of the priceless artefacts once owned by the dukes of Courland, and another dedicated to medieval religious art hidden from the Soviets during their occupation of Latvia. The French garden behind the palace is open to the public in the summer.

Mežotne Palace

Seldom visited, **Mežotnes pils** (Mežotne Palace) often plays second fiddle to Rundāle, but is in fact one of the nation's most impressive late 18th-century architectural monuments. The manor was a gift from Catherine the

Great to Charlotte von Lieven, her grandchildren's tutor, who was later bestowed with the title of countess. Unfortunately, the neo-classical palace was badly damaged during the wars of the 20th century, and the graves of soldiers in the English garden are a testament to these turbulent times. Mežotne has now been completely renovated and converted into a hotel, although it is still open to the public for tours. If you have the time and the inclination, you can spend the night here for a fraction of the cost of accommodation in Old Riga.

Above: Bauska Castle
Right: Rundāle Palace

Leisure
Activities

SHOPPING

Riga has no shortage of retail outlets selling almost anything that's available in other European capitals, but bear in mind that imported goods such as clothing and electronics can be prohibitively expensive. Fortunately, most visitors are more likely to buy an amber necklace than a washing machine, so shopping here can be a real treat for bargain hunters. Latvian crafts such as linen tablecloths, ceramics and local jewellery may not be as cheap as they used to be, but they're still relatively inexpensive when compared with similar goods sold in other EU countries.

Prices at shops should be regarded as set in stone, but it may be possible to do a little haggling with vendors at souvenir stalls and at the Central Market. Non-European Union citizens can take advantage of opportunities to shop tax free, which can amount to a tidy saving, especially when one considers that the VAT rate in Latvia is 18 percent. You must purchase at least 59Ls worth of goods from one participating shop and ask for a tax-free cheque, which you then present at customs at the airport, ferry port or at land border crossings. After this is stamped, you can go to the refund office at the aforementioned departure points and receive your money. If leaving by train, you can send your stamped cheque to the tax-free authorities in Latvia by mail.

There is no designated shopping district in Riga, but as a general rule many antique and souvenir shops are located in the old town, while clothing and shoe shops tend to be situated on the main streets of A. Čaka, K. Barona, Tērbatas and Brīvības. Trendy shopping malls with hundreds of shops are located on the periphery of the city, where there is much more room for parking and further development. Credit and bank cards are widely accepted in Riga, and most shops are open 10am–7pm on weekdays and 11am–5pm on Saturdays and many are closed on Sunday. Major shopping centres usually open daily 10am–10pm.

Markets

The **Central Market** (Prāgas 1; open daily 8am–6pm) is the most picturesque place to shop in Riga, and you can purchase anything that's in season from local berries and mushrooms from the surrounding forests to imported kiwis. The Norwegian chain of supermarkets, **Rimi** (Stacijas laukums 2; 10am–10pm), has several shops in the city centre, but by far the best place to buy groceries is **Stockmann** (13 Janvāra 8; 9am–10pm), where you can buy goods ranging from freshly baked bread and Campbell's soup to *filet mignon* and pre-packaged curry sauce.

Shopping centres

As recently as 1995 there was only one major shopping centre in the entire city; now they're too numerous to count. The **Centrs** shopping centre (Audēju 16; open daily 10am–10pm) is conveniently located in Old Riga and offers four floors of retail space, but if a mere few dozen shops don't grab your attention, then take a short bus ride to **Mols** (Krasta 46; open daily 10am–10pm), which is probably the closest thing Latvia has to an American mall. The train station has basically been converted into a giant

Left: traditional costume
Right: Laima chocolates, made in Latvia since 1925

shopping centre called **Origo** (Stacijas laukums 2; open 10am–10pm), which is also a convenient option.

Antiques

Shops selling antiques abound in Old Riga and in the city centre. Books in German and Russian, the old languages of the empire, as well as in Latvian, can be found at **Jumava** (R. Vāgnera 12; open Mon–Fri 10am–6pm, Sat 10am–5pm). Religious icons are a very popular item at most antiques shops, but bear in mind that the painting of Jesus you're about to purchase may have a congregation that's still looking for it. Ask the seller if the particular icon you wish to buy has any paperwork that guarantees its authenticity and its legal status. The best place for icons is **Volmar** (Šķūņu 6; open Mon–Fri 10am–8pm, Sun 11am–6pm), located close to Dome Square.

Soviet memorabilia is another hot area of collecting, and nearly every shop has some old military medals, worthless roubles or perhaps even a bust of Lenin. Cramped and crowded, the **Galerija** (Dzirnavu 53; Mon–Fri 10am–7pm, Sat 11am–5pm) and **Retro A**

(Tallinas 54; open Mon–Fri 10am–5pm, Sat 10am–2pm) have a decent selection of Cold War-era communist nick-nacks.

For old lithographs, furniture and fine art, try **Antiqua** (Vaļņu 25; open Mon–Fri noon–7pm, Sat 11am–3pm) in Old Riga.

Many shops also sell antique cameras, so be on the lookout for the elusive Minox spy camera that was designed and manufactured in Riga.

Amber

Latvia has been a source of amber since ancient times, and the Roman historian Tacitus (55–117) described the mythology of the Latvians and their land on the 'Amber Sea' in his writings. Anyone who has been to a beach in Latvia knows how close the pine trees are to the shore, and it is the petrified sap of these trees from a bygone era that has been washed up on the Baltic coast for millennia. Amber comes in a variety of colours from a murky yellowish-white to dark brown. The most prized pieces are clear and honey-coloured, and are made even more valuable if they have a prehistoric insect or leaf trapped inside.

Amber is available in nearly every souvenir shop in town and is sold by vendors on Līvu laukums and on Vaļņu and Skārņu streets. Some of the most impressive examples can be found at **Dzintara galerija** (Torņa 4; open Mon–Sat 10am–7pm, Sun 11am–5pm) and **Dzintara muzejs** (Kalēju 9–11; open daily 11am–7pm).

Silver Jewellery

Many shops around town sell silver rings, necklaces and earrings based on ancient Baltic designs found at archaeological excavation sites around the country. The woven rope-like ring that nearly every Latvian possesses is called a *Namejs,* named after a 13th-century tribal chieftain who retreated to Lithuania rather than be conquered by German crusaders. Legend has it that he left his ring with his son, but that the invaders found out and began scouring the countryside in search of a man with this particular item of jewellery. To protect the Namejs family, men everywhere started to wearing a similar ring in order to confuse the Germans.

Left: amber stalls

For silver jewellery, pay a visit to **Tornis** (Grēcinieku 11; open Mon–Sat 10am–6pm, Sun 10am–4pm; www.balturotas.lv), located next to St Peter's Church, and **Līvs** (Kalēju 7; open Mon–Fri 10am–6pm, Sat 10am–4pm), which also has a great selection of linens and hand-woven blankets.

Linen

If tourists can't seem to visit the Middle East without buying an Oriental carpet, then the same is true for the linen tablecloth in Latvia. Practical, beautiful and easily packed into a suitcase, it is the ideal gift or souvenir. For traditional styles, visit **Tīne** (Vaļņu 2; open Mon–Sat 9am–7pm, Sun 10am–5pm), which also offers nearly every kind of souvenir possible from woollen socks to postcards; **Senā klēts** (Merķeļa 13; open Mon–Fri 10am–6pm, Sat 10am–4pm), which specialises in Latvian folk costumes; and, for contemporary linens and non-traditional gifts, try **Grieži** (Mazā Miesnieku 1; open Mon–Fri 11am–7pm; Sat 11am–6pm).

Alcohol and Chocolates

Latvijas Balzams produces dozens of brandies, whiskeys, vodkas and liqueurs, not to mention the infamous national drink *Rīgas Melnais Balzams*, a bitter black herbal concoction made of 25 different ingredients bottled in a ceramic jug. Latvijas Balzams shops are found all over town and they also sell T-shirts – another great souvenir.

Inexpensive and delicious, **Laima chocolates** are exported all over Europe and have been produced in Latvia since 1925. They are available at all supermarkets, most convenience stores and kiosks as well as at dozens of Laima shops throughout Riga.

Music

This always makes a good gift, and Riga's pedigree as home to Richard Wagner and Eurovision superstar Marie N. is reason enough to buy a local CD. The Latvian Folk Music Collection series produced by the Upe Recording Studio is a good place to start. Each CD in the series is based on a theme such as Latvian dances, songs about war, and songs about beer. The disc of Latvian lullabies is a perfect present for parents with small children. Albums by Skandinieki and Iļģi are also recommended. Recordings of the Song and Dance Festival held every five years *(see page 83)*, and of organ concerts at the Dome Cathedral, are also good choices. For those who prefer something more modern, try Latvia's most renowned pop band, Brainstorm.

Above: traditional woollen socks
Right: making chocolate

But Latvians have plenty of other culinary treats to offer, including some of the best bread you may ever taste. Although white bread is becoming more popular, the older generation will scoff at it, considering it a snack or even a dessert. Real Latvian bread is made from rye (called *rupjmaize*) or from a combination of wheat and rye (called *saldskābmaize* – sweet and sour bread), which is arguably the most delicious. The dark hue of the bread is achieved by using only natural ingredients and never by food colouring or syrups.

Pastries called *pīrāgi* are also national treasures. The little buns filled with ham and onions, sauerkraut, minced meat or a variety of other ingredients can be found in most local supermarkets, bakeries and cafés. Grey peas, or *pelēkie zirņi* in Latvian, fried with bacon and onions are another favourite and are often topped with sour cream or *kefīrs*, a dairy drink similar to yoghurt or buttermilk, that is definitely an acquired taste.

Although dozens of varieties of sausages are made in Latvia, many include a hefty dose of caraway seeds, not to mention large pieces of fat and gristle. Your best bet is to try either *mednieku desiņas*, thin hunters' sausages, or *asinsdesa*, blood sausages, usually served with lingonberry sauce.

Thankfully, Riga's dining scene has evolved by leaps and bounds since the fall of communism, so you can have pancakes at an American diner for breakfast, *tekkamaki* rolls at a sushi bar for lunch and nouvelle cuisine at a trendy fusion restaurant for dinner – all at a fraction of the cost of similar establishments in Western Europe. Although many restaurants stay open until all hours of the night, kitchens usually close by 11pm.

The following key is a list of price ranges for the cost of a main course only.

$$$$	7–10Ls
$$$	5–7Ls
$$	3–5Ls
$	under 3Ls

EATING OUT

Although one might think that centuries of domination by several different foreign powers would have had a positive effect on local cuisine, bear in mind that the Germans, Swedes, Poles and Russians didn't have much to offer on the culinary front. Therefore, Latvian cuisine usually consists of the two Ps: pork and potatoes. These two basic ingredients are rarely complete, however, without a heavy cream sauce, delicious wild mushrooms and a generous sprinkling of dill or caraway seeds, the only 'spices' known or accepted by Latvian grandmothers.

On the bright side, it would certainly be difficult to find a better *karbonāde*, a pork chop or schnitzel, outside Latvia. The nation's favourite white meat is served in a variety of ways, all of which are delicious. In fact, pig meat is so revered that the snout and ears are served as a delicacy, especially at Christmas.

Latvian

Alus Ordenis
Raiņa 15
Tel: 781 41 90
This beer cellar and restaurant serves Latvia's best brew *Užavas* in large ceramic mugs and

Above: alfresco cocktails

tasty, artery-clogging local cuisine such as pork ribs and potatoes, fried herring and even 'bulls' glands' for the more adventurous. Menus are conveniently available in English and German. **$$**

Lambetvoks
Lāčplēša 12
Tel: 728 92 55
Named after the *Lambeth Walk*, the English song that was popular in 1930s' Riga, this cosy restaurant housed in a restored 19th-century wooden house has successfully captured the atmosphere of interwar Latvia. Inexpensive Latvian food, drink and music are all available here, as well as a fireplace for cold winter nights and occasional live piano concerts. **$$**

Staburags
A. Čaka 55
Tel: 729 97 87
This is without a doubt the best place in the city centre to have an authentic Latvian dining experience. It's a labyrinth of hidden niches and dining halls on different levels, all decorated to look like a country farmstead. No trip here is complete without a local beer served in litre mugs, or in wooden kegs brought to your table, and do try pigs' legs with sauerkraut and potatoes – the house speciality. The ceramic jugs on each table are for discarded bones, not flowers. Cash only. **$$**

Ethnic

El Čarlito
Blaumaņa 38–40 (entrance from Pērses)
Tel: 777 05 72
If you're looking for casual dining and Tex-Mex food then seek no further than El Čarlito, which offers the city's best fajitas and a perpetual fiesta atmosphere. In the summer, the large courtyard is transformed into a big barbecue that is just a sombrero short of a beach party in Cabo. Cold Coronas and tequila shots are always plentiful. **$$**

Indian Raja
Vecpilsētas 3
Tel: 721 26 14
Although many ethnic restaurants in Riga fall far short of the mark, Indian Raja is refreshingly authentic. Located in a cosy brick cellar that was used to store exotic spices in medieval times, its delicious curries, tandoori and vindaloo dishes are guaranteed to make your mouth water. Locals who prefer bland food seldom dine here, so it relies almost entirely on tourists and local expats to make ends meet. **$$$$**

Kabuki
K. Barona 14 (entrance from Elizabetes)
Tel: 728 20 52
www.kabuki.lv
This modern sushi restaurant is so stylish that it would have no problem holding its own in New York, London or Tokyo. The grey minimalist interior is offset by waiting staff dressed in shiny silk kimonos and by colourful sushi chefs behind the bar. You can dine by the large picture windows and people-watch or take a seat next to the conveyor belt and sample whatever passes. **$$$$**

Nostaļģija
Kaļķu 22
Tel: 722 23 38
It appears that at least a few people are capable of making light of the Soviet occupation of Latvia. This glitzy dining hall is decorated with communist murals of the proletariat performing various tasks, and although most locals wouldn't be caught dead here, it's popular among tourists searching for a glimpse of the past. Slavic cuisine is available as well as decadent dishes from the imperialist West. **$$**

Spotikačs
Antonijas 12
Tel: 750 59 55
This kitsch restaurant, which serves delicious Ukrainian cuisine, looks like an exhibit at an ethnographic museum. Start with the borscht served with a side dish of fresh biscuits and hot pepper oil or the potato dumplings called *vareniki*, then move on to tasty pork and chicken main courses. In case you're wondering, *Spotikačs* is the Latvian name of a traditional homemade fruit vodka. **$$**

International

Charlestons
Blaumaņa 38–40
Tel: 777 05 73

A good place to impress both friends and business associates, Charlestons provides fine dining at a reasonable price. Owned by local celebrity and renowned Latvian-Canadian restaurateur Elmārs Tannis, it's a classic European restaurant with North American flare. Order a delicious steak in the main dining hall or an omelette at the breakfast bar. $$$

Fabrikas restorāns
Balasta dambis 70
Tel: 787 38 04
Don't be discouraged by its location on the left bank of the river. This stylish restaurant, in a renovated factory that now houses luxury apartments, offers excellent views of Old Riga and delicious fusion and international cuisine at reasonable prices. In the summer, you can dine outdoors by the water and watch sailboats and cruise ships drift by at the nearby port. $$$

Light
Dzirnavu 84/1 (Berga Bazārs)
Tel: 728 14 20
This trendy restaurant has become a real favourite of locals, who want good food, great people-watching opportunities and reasonable prices. The menu is a combination of international and fusion dishes from *al dente* pasta to politically incorrect sturgeon fillets. Don't leave without trying the homemade spring rolls, which are simply fabulous. $$

Macaroni Noodle Bar
K. Barona 17
Tel: 721 79 81
The name puts one in mind of cheap fast-food noodle stalls in Bangkok or Hong Kong, but this noodle bar is actually a trendy restaurant that is packed with smartly dressed businessmen and women in the day and the upmarket cocktail crowd at night. Different pasta dishes created from recipes collected by the chef on his travels around the world are on offer, but keep in mind that the size of the servings leans towards those of nouvelle cuisine. $$$

Melnie mūki
Jāņa sēta 1 (entrance from Kalēju)
Tel: 721 50 06
The Black Monks is located in what used to be a convent, and its romantic red brick walls are a testament to its ancient monastic past. It's the perfect place for a candlelit date or just dinner with friends, and its menu is so extensive that it would take you the better part of an hour to read it from cover to cover. Reservations essential in the evenings. $$

Vanilla Café
Vaļņu 26
Tel: 722 14 35
Modern, trendy and very brown, Vanilla Café is a place to see and be seen. The ground floor offers fusion cuisine as well as sushi and a more relaxed atmosphere, while the first floor is reserved for people who don't mind spending 40Ls per person for dinner. $$$–$$$$

Above: camomile and garlic

Medieval

Pie Kristapa kunga
Baznīcas 27/29
Tel: 729 48 99
According to the legend dreamt up by the owners of this kitsch restaurant, Kristaps was a crusader who travelled to the Holy Land and beyond before settling here in Riga. You can now eat in his house and admire his collection of antiques. The menu offers Latvian, European, Russian and Armenian cuisine, the beer selection is excellent, and the prices are reasonable. You can also smoke a hookah in the Eastern room or pick a live fish from the cellar 'pond' for dinner. **$$**

Rozengrāls
Rozena 1
Tel: 722 47 48
www.rozengrals.lv
Housed in a 13th-century vaulted brick cellar that was once used for feasts by the town hall, Rozengrāls offers authentic medieval food and drink served by waiting staff in period costume. Potatoes, tomatoes and any other ingredients not available in Middle Age Latvia are absent from the menu, and many of the recipes used here are from ancient cookbooks. **$$$$**

Vegetarian

Kamāla
Jauniela 14
Tel: 721 13 32
A vegetarian restaurant located here in pork country seemed doomed to failure, but years later Kamāla is still serving Asian-style rice, lentils and vegetable dishes to a growing number of Latvians concerned about animal rights and their health. Incense, Indian music and ornately carved wooden furniture complete the experience. **$$**

Rāma
K. Barona 56
Tel: 727 24 90
Run by the local Riga chapter of the Hare Krishnas, this small café serves tasty vegetarian Indian cuisine at ridiculously low prices. Proceeds fund their soup kitchen for the homeless, so you can eat a spicy, healthy meal and support a good cause at the same time. Cash only. **$**

Upmarket

Bergs
Elizabetes 83–85 (Berga Bazārs)
Tel: 777 09 49
www.hotelbergs.lv
Leave behind any prejudices you might have towards hotel restaurants, because Bergs shatters the myth that they lack ambience and only serve bland food to tourists. The décor is like something from a design magazine, the service is outstanding, and the ever-changing menu of gourmet cuisine is unparalleled in Riga. Reservations recommended. *See also page 90.* **$$$$**

Vincents
Elizabetes 19
Tel: 733 26 34
Renowned chef Mārtiņš Rītiņš has served gourmet cuisine to world-famous actors, pop stars, billionaire businessmen, heads of state and even royalty over the years, so why not see for yourself what all the fuss is about. **$$$$**

Left: wild mushrooms
Right: *grūdenis* is a thick country stew that uses half a pig's head

alone, but it is also the venue for world-class opera and ballet performances. Tickets are often ridiculously inexpensive, but seats do sell out, so buy them as soon as possible. For programme details, visit www.opera.lv.

No trip to Riga is complete without taking in an **organ concert** at Dome Cathedral. Once the world's largest organ, it never fails to impress, and many professional musicians from around the globe waive their fees just for a chance to perform here. The Wagner Concert Hall is a great venue for classical music and it has the added distinction of having had Richard Wagner as its conductor from 1837–39. Finally, the Great Guild is home to the **Latvian Symphony Orchestra**, another excellent venue for classical music. For up-to-date listings of concerts and events pick up a copy of *Riga In Your Pocket,* available at hotels, bookshops and kiosks around town.

Riga also offers several cinemas that show a wide variety of films, from Hollywood blockbusters to European art-house films. Films are always shown in their original language with subtitles in both Latvian and Russian. Forum Cinemas *(see below)* is home to the second-largest movie screen in Northern Europe.

Cinemas

Daile
K. Barona 31
Tel: 728 38 54
Offers Hollywood films at discounted rates roughly a month after they have premiered at the larger Forum Cinemas.

Forum Cinemas
13 janvāra 8
www.forumcinemas.lv
The largest cinema in Latvia with 14 different auditoriums showing blockbuster films.

K. Suns
Elizabetes 83–85
Tel: 728 54 11
A small cinema showing arty films.

Riga
Elizabetes 61
Tel: 728 11 05
Riga's oldest cinema offers a combination of foreign and Hollywood movies.

NIGHTLIFE

Riga prides itself on its dynamic, no holds-barred nightlife, and it's often for this reason that many Brits and Germans make the journey on low-cost airlines from London or Berlin to the Latvian capital. Beer is relatively cheap by Western standards, and the city has a reputation for having some of the most beautiful women in the world. Add to this the fact that many **pubs** and **clubs** don't close their doors if patrons are still willing to spend money, no matter what the hour, and the tempting presence of dozens of 24-hour casinos and gaming halls offering free drinks to their customers, and you have a recipe for hedonism.

For those seeking more refined entertainment opportunities, Riga has no shortage of musical concerts. The city's 19th-century **opera house** is worth a visit for its opulence

Above: interior of the National Opera House

Concert Halls

Doma baznīca
Doma laukums 1
Tel: 721 32 13
The best venue for organ concerts.

Lielā ģilde
Amatu 6
Tel: 721 37 98
Home of the Latvian Symphony Orchestra.

Latvijas Nacionālā opera
Aspazijas bulvāris 3
Tel: 707 37 77
www.opera.lv
The opera house puts on opera and ballet performances as well as concerts by a variety of major international stars.

Mazā ģilde
Amatu 3/5
Tel: 722 37 72
Chamber music concerts and special events are often held here.

Vāgnera koncertzāle
R. Vāgnera 4
Tel: 721 08 17
Classical music concerts are held at this venue, where the composer Richard Wagner once conducted.

Theatre

Dailes teātris
Brīvības 75
Tel: 727 02 78
Shows both traditional and contemporary theatrical productions in Latvian.

Latvijas Nacionālais teātris
Kronvalda bulvāris 2
Tel: 732 27 59
Traditional theatre in Latvian.

Jaunais Rīgas teātris
Lāčplēša 25
Tel: 728 07 65
www.jrt.lv
Avant-garde theatre performances.

Krievu drāmas teātris
Kaļķu 16
Tel: 722 46 60

Traditional and modern theatre putting on dramatic works in Russian.

Live Music

Austrumu Robeža
R. Vāgnera 8 (entrance from Gleznotāju)
Tel: 781 42 02
Decorated like a World War II bunker with both Soviet and Nazi paraphernalia, the 'Eastern Border' is a clever 'homage' to Latvia's former occupiers. The scene of poetry readings and impromptu skits, it also hosts local country, bluegrass and rock bands.

Bites Blūzs Klubs
Dzirnavu 34a
Tel: 733 31 25
The only venue for live blues in Riga, this small club often flies over acts from destinations as far away as Chicago and Memphis. It also serves excellent, albeit pricey, international-style cuisine.

Četri Balti Krekli
Vecpilsētas 12
Tel: 721 38 85
www.krekli.lv
Named after a famous film, this brick cellar in Old Riga has made a pledge to its patrons to only play Latvian music, hence its immense popularity. This is the place to see live local rock acts. Men must wear proper shoes, as anyone with trainers will be barred entrance.

Kabata
Peldu 19
Tel: 722 33 34

Right: lavish operatic production

This sprawling brick cellar with medieval vaulted ceilings is a popular place for 20-somethings to dance to chart hits; it also hosts frequent rock concerts by local artists.

Kreisais Pagrieziens
Kaļķu 11a
Tel: 721 25 75
A venue for a more mature crowd, 'The Left Turn' has hosted concerts by such local luminaries as Ainars Mielavs and Eurovision Song Contest winner, Marie N.

Liize Jazz Bar
Vecpilsētas 19
Tel: 749 09 65
This cosy cellar bar offers classic jazz performances in Old Riga as well as tasty international food for lunch and dinner.

Sapnu Fabrika
Lāčplēša 101
Tel: 729 17 01
With a name that means the 'Dream Factory', this is a renovated warehouse in the city centre. It has hosted concerts by many international stars, including the White Stripes.

Bars and Pubs
A. Suns
Elizabetes 83–85 (Berga Bazārs)
Tel: 728 84 18
This smoky, industrial-style café and late-night watering hole is popular with expats and locals. The international cuisine isn't exactly great value for money, but most people come here for drinks and the chance to socialise.

Dickens
Grēcinieku 9/1
Tel: 721 30 87
www.dickens.lv
Dickens is *the* destination for the city's expatriates and tourists. With dozens of foreign and domestic beers on draught, a proper English breakfast and the best fish and chips in town, it's almost always packed full of thirsty patrons.

Orange Bar
Jāņa sēta 5
Tel: 722 84 23
www.orangebar.lv
The city's only bar that is completely dedicated to alternative music, it rarely sees an evening without boozy 20-somethings dancing on the tabletops.

Paddy Whelan's
Grēcinieku 4
Tel: 721 02 49
Riga's first Irish pub opened its doors in 1995 and has been a staple of the city's nightlife scene ever since. However, competition from new rivals has forced Paddy's to rethink its business plan, and it has transformed itself into the best sports bar in town, with dozens of flat screen TVs showing live sporting events from English Premiership football to American baseball.

Above: one of Riga's many chic bars

Runcis
Jāņa sēta 1
Tel: 722 41 98
It's almost a pity to mention this classic Old Riga pub that seldom sees foreigners or even local Russian-speakers for that matter. Smoky and a little bit rough around the edges, it serves only cheap Latvian food and drink and is a favourite of card players and others out for a quiet drink in relative anonymity.

Tim McShane's
Tirgoņu 10
Tel: 722 24 38
A converted 17th-century warehouse in Old Riga is the perfect place for a cosy Irish pub. What it lacks in culinary skills, it more than makes up for in its unparalleled beer selecon – the largest in the city.

Discos

Club Essential
Skolas 2
Tel: 724 22 89
www.essential.lv
Renowned DJs from around Europe often perform here on weekend nights making Club Essential one of the most popular dance venues in town.

La Rocca
Brīvības 96
Tel: 750 60 30
www.larocca.lv
The largest dance club in Riga also offers an exclusive strip club and casino. Expect beautiful people dressed to perfection and loud techno music.

Nautilus
Kungu 8
Tel: 781 44 77
www.nautilus.lv
Considered to be one of the best clubs in the city, Nautilus is vaguely reminiscent of the hold of a submarine and waitresses wear sexy sailor suits.

Pulkvedis
Peldu 26–28
Tel: 721 38 86
www.pulkvedis.lv

Filled with a loyal crowd of arty types and bohemians, this has been one of Riga's top clubs since 1995. The industrial-style ground floor has a central circular bar and a small dance floor and the retro cellar bar looks like a scene from an Austin Powers film.

Casinos

A recent Latvian law requires that everyone must register his or her passport or ID card upon entering a casino.

Tobago
Aspazijas 22 (entrance from Vaļņu)
Tel: 722 22 85
A 24-hour casino, where the staff dress in pirate costumes.

Tower Voodoo Casino
Elizabetes 55
Tel: 777 22 85
www.tower.lv
Roulette, poker, blackjack and all of the usual casino games are on offer.

Gay Riga

Although the city is far from gay-friendly (participants of the first gay pride parade were pelted with eggs and fruit by religious zealots and homophobes), it does support a growing, vibrant homosexual nightlife scene.

XXL
A. Kalniņa 4
Tel: 728 22 76
www.xxl.lv
The classiest gay club in town is decorated with risqué artwork by a famous gay artist from Finland.

Right: inside Nautilus

The colours and patterns are transferred to the eggs to create unique designs. It is also traditional to decorate eggs with ancient pagan symbols.

Christmas is celebrated with gusto, especially since it was outlawed as recently as 20 years ago. A crafts fair is held each year on one of Old Riga's squares, usually Dome or Livs', and concerts and special events are organised there throughout the whole of December. Latvians eat grey peas for good luck on New Year's Eve and also engage in fortune telling by pouring molten lead into cold water. The shape is then analysed by an 'expert', and your future is foretold.

Most traditional celebrations can be experienced first-hand at the Open-Air Ethnographic Museum (20 minutes away from Riga on the No. 1 bus from Tērbatas; open 10am–5pm; admission fee), where Latvians in national costumes act out ancient rituals on the equinoxes and solstices.

The next Latvian Song and Dance Festival will take place in the summer of 2008. The festival has been held roughly every four or five years since 1873, and its highlight is the final concert during which hundreds of choirs sing in front of tens of thousands of spectators. Although the dates have been changed over the years, for the sake of convenience, the organisers have promised that the event will now occur every five years.

CALENDAR OF EVENTS

Nearly 800 years of occupation by foreign powers has given the Latvians little cause for celebration, so holidays usually revolve around ancient pre-Christian pagan customs or tragic past events. The nation's largest and most eagerly awaited holiday is Midsummer's Eve – Līgo and Jāņ – held on 23–24 June. Latvians decorate their cars with oak leaves and head out to the countryside for bonfires and late-night drinking, after stopping to buy copious amounts of beer, meat for grilling and insect repellent. Latvians claim that if you sleep on the summer solstice you'll sleep for the rest of the summer, so everyone attempts to stay awake until sunrise. Locals jump over the bonfire three times for luck and search for the mythical fern flower, or *papardes zieds*, out in the woods with their significant others. The elusive flora doesn't exist, but it is after all an ancient fertility festival.

Most Latvians are either Lutheran, Catholic or Orthodox Christians – at least nominally – so Easter is another major holiday often celebrated by families at home or with close friends. Eggs are placed in little sacks with onion skins, flowers and pine needles and then boiled in water.

April

The **International Baltic Ballet Festival** is held each April and features the best performers from Northern Europe. The **Bimini International Animated Film Festival** is held at the Riga Cinema each year.

May

Hockey is a national obsession, and many businesses close early each May to allow their employees to watch the Latvians strive for glory at the IIHF **World Hockey Championship**. In 2006 Riga will host the event, which should spark great interest in the city.

June

An annual crafts fair called **Gadatirgus** is held at the Open-Air Ethnographic Museum on the first weekend of June each year. A

Above: celebrating Midsummer's Eve. **Right:** folk dancers in Dome Square

crafts fair called **Zāļu tirgus** is held on Dome Square on 22 June, the day before Midsummer's Eve. **Midsummer's Eve** is celebrated on 23–24 June.

The **Riga Opera Festival** is held at the National Opera and takes place each year for roughly two weeks in June. Renowned international stars from around the world often participate. The **Rīgas Ritmi Rhythmic Music Festival** is held at various venues around the city each June. International R&B and Latin-style bands take part in the festival.

July

An annual **Organ Music Festival** is held each year at Dome Cathedral.

August

Every year musicians from around Europe participate in the **Riga Sacred Music Festival**, held in churches across the city.

September

Each year on the last Saturday of September, a **harvest festival** is held on Dome and Town Hall squares. Food, drink and craft stalls help the festivities along. Other cultural festivals include the **International Chamber Music Festival**, usually held in September, and the **Baltic Pearl International Film Festival**, held each September. The **Homo Novus International Festival of Contemporary Theatre** also takes place in Riga every two years at the end of September.

October

The **Arena New Music Festival** is held each year in October with international stars performing at venues across the city.

November

Lāčplēsis Day is commemorated each year on 11 November by Riga Castle, where hundreds of people light candles to honour the memory of Latvia's fallen heroes. Latvians also light candles at home and place them by a window so they can be seen outside.

A variety of events and concerts are held each year on 18 November, **Latvian Independence Day**. A military parade is held in the afternoon followed by the singing of patriotic songs at the Freedom Monument.

December

Christmas concerts, food and drink stalls and a crafts market are held on Livs' or Dome Square every December.

Practical Information

GETTING THERE

By Air

The national carrier airBaltic (www.air baltic.com), which is partially owned by Scandinavian Airlines-SAS, offers affordable direct flights to Riga from London, Dublin, Brussels, Berlin, Stockholm and several other cities in Europe. Thankfully, low-cost airlines have also recently opened up direct routes to Riga. Ryanair (www.ryanair.com) runs flights from London Stansted, Liverpool, Frankfurt Hahn, Stockholm Skavsta and Tampere (Finland), while rivals easyJet (www.easyjet.com) fly from Berlin Shoenefeld. The following airlines also operate flights to Riga from their local hubs: British Airways (London Heathrow), KLM (Amsterdam), Lufthansa (Frankfurt and Munich), Finnair (Helsinki), Aeroflot (Moscow Sheremetevo), Czech Airlines (Prague), Austrian Airlines (Vienna) and LOT Polish Airlines (Warsaw).

If travelling from North America, contact Scandinavian Airlines-SAS, British Airways, KLM, Lufthansa, Finnair, Czech Airlines or LOT Polish Airlines for the most convenient connections, or try Uzbekistan Airways (235 W 48 Broadway, New York; tel: 212-245 10 05; www.uzairways.com), which offers direct flights from New York to Riga twice a week. If you are travelling from Australia or New Zealand, try British Airways or Lufthansa.

By Rail

It is possible to reach Latvia by rail, but the number of times you must change trains discourages most people from attempting the trip. An express train linking Berlin and St Petersburg, with stops in Kaliningrad and Riga, began service in 2006.

By Road

Eurolines (www.eurolines.lv) offers bus connections to cities throughout Europe, including London.

Left: St John's Courtyard
Right: Riga's coat-of-arms, Small Guild

By Sea

Ferry services to Riga are available every other day from Stockholm. For more information visit www.rigasealine.lv. It is also possible to travel to other Latvian cities such as Liepāja and Ventspils from Lübeck (www. latlines.lv) and Rostock (Terrabalt Company, tel: 342 72 14), Germany and Karlshamn (Terrabalt Company, tel: 342 72 14) and Nynashamn (www.scandlines.lv), Sweden.

By Car

The border crossings with Latvia's European Union (EU) neighbours are usually swift and hassle-free. Passenger vehicles can drive past the queue of lorries waiting to clear customs.

TRAVEL ESSENTIALS

When to Visit

The best time to visit Riga is in summer between mid-May and mid-September. Winters are often wet and harsh with very little sunlight increasing the gloom – perhaps why Latvia has the fifth-highest rate of suicide in the world. It's not uncommon for Riga to experience snow flurries as late as April.

Visas and Passports

Citizens of the EU, Andorra, Australia, Bulgaria, Canada, Costa Rica, Croatia, Iceland, Israel, Japan, Liechtenstein, Monaco, New Zealand, Nicaragua, Romania, the SAR of

Electricity

Like the rest of continental Europe, the electrical current used in Latvia is 220V AC, 50Hz. Two-pronged European-style plugs are used.

Time Differences

Latvia is in the Eastern European time zone, which is GMT + 2 hours. An hour is added or subtracted at the end of March and October for daylight savings time, and local time is GMT + 3 hours during the summer – known as Eastern European Summer Time or EEST for short.

GETTING ACQUAINTED

Geography

Riga straddles the River Daugava, which ends at the Baltic Sea approximately 10 km (6 miles) downstream of the city centre. Parkland comprises nearly 20 percent of Riga's 307-sq km (118-sq mile) area.

Government and Economy

Not unlike many of the other former Soviet-bloc nations that have now become fully fledged members of the EU, Latvia has experienced an economic boom since regaining independence in 1991, especially in the property market and construction industry. Unfortunately, EU accession also heralded a dramatic rise in inflation, which may delay Latvian plans to adopt the euro in 2008.

The Latvian parliament or *saeima* is comprised of 100 deputies, who are elected every four years. The president, who appoints the prime minister, is the nation's official head of state and is elected by the parliament for a four-year term. Latvia's current president, Vaira Vīķe-Freiberga, has been in power since 1999. Sadly, political in-fighting and partisanship have led to the demise of 11 governments in nearly as many years.

Religion

Christianity replaced the ancient pagan animistic religion of Latvia in the 13th and 14th centuries. Since the Reformation Lutheranism has been the country's dominant religion,

Hong Kong, South Korea, Switzerland, Uruguay, US and Vatican City may enter Latvia without a visa and stay up to 90 days every six months. Citizens of all other nationalities/states require a visa.

Vaccinations

You do not need any special vaccinations to enter Latvia, but cases of tick-borne encephalitis are not uncommon in the countryside. It should also be mentioned that the World Health Organisation has named the Baltic States as a hot zone for drug-resistant strains of tuberculosis.

Customs

Travellers are permitted to bring in 2 litres of wine, 1 litre of spirits and 5 litres of beer as well as 200 cigarettes or 20 cigars. There are no limits on the amount of currency you may bring with you into Latvia.

Clothing

Temperatures of -20°C (-4°F) are not uncommon during the winter months, so bring a hat, gloves, warm coat and perhaps thermal underwear. A light raincoat or windbreaker will come in handy in spring and summer, and warm clothing is essential in autumn. Evening wear is expected at the opera, and some nightclubs will bar admittance to clubbers in trainers, so bring a pair of more formal shoes if going out.

Above: manhole cover designed for Riga's 800-year anniversary

although Orthodox Christianity and Catholicism are also widely practised, especially in eastern Latvia. Riga is also home to one of the oldest surviving groups of Old Believers in the world. Judaism in Latvia was all but destroyed by the Nazis during World War II. The Soviets persecuted clerics and followers of any religion, and many of the nation's historic places of worship were converted into concert halls and museums. Since independence, churches have been restored and returned to their ever-growing congregations.

How Not To Offend
Having nearly become a minority in their own nation due to the russification policies of the Soviets, Latvians are extremely proud of their cultural traditions and their language. Although tolerated, Russian is usually spoken reluctantly by Latvians. English is widely spoken in the capital.

Population
According to the official census, the population of Riga is 747,200. Due to the russification policies of the Soviets, Russian-speakers (Russians, Ukrainians, Belarussians and others) slightly outnumber Latvians in the capital city. Nearly one third of the nation's inhabitants live in Riga.

MONEY MATTERS

Currency
In 1993 the lat replaced the transitional Latvian rouble, becoming one of the world's most valuable currencies – worth roughly the same amount as the British pound. One lat (Lt) consists of 100 santīmi, with 1, 2, 5, 10, 20 and 50 santīmi and 1 and 2 lat coins. Bank notes are available in denominations of 5, 10, 20, 50, 100 and 500 lats. Although Latvia is now a member of the EU, it's not expected to adopt the euro until 2008 at the earliest.

Credit Cards
Cash is still the preferred method of payment in Latvia, but most hotels, restaurants, many shops and even taxis accept major credit and bank cards.

Cash Machines
ATMs, known locally as *bankomāti*, are located on nearly every street corner in Old Riga and the city centre and accept all major credit and bank cards.

Tipping
Latvians are warming up to the idea of tipping, but many still only round up to the nearest lat. Foreigners, however, are generally expected to leave an additional 10 percent for good service, and some menus do warn customers that a gratuity will be automatically added to the bill.

Taxes
A steep value-added tax of 18 percent is included in the price of all items at shops and restaurants. A lower tax of 5 percent is included in all hotel bills.

Money Changers
Currency exchanges, some open 24 hours, are widely available, especially in Old Riga, but rates differ little from those at banks. Hotels, casinos and even some shops also exchange money. You should always check the rates before exchanging any money, but unlike major tourist destinations in Europe, scams and wildly differing rates are rare.

Travellers' Cheques
Establishments accepting travellers' cheques are less common, but you can cash them at most banks. After business hours the only place to cash travellers' cheques is the Radisson SAS Daugava Hotel on the left bank of the river.

GETTING AROUND

Taxis
Like cabs in most cities, taxis in Riga can be both dodgy and reputable. Respectable firms should charge the official tariff, which is 0.40Ls for pick up and 0.30Ls per each additional kilometre during the day, or 0.60Ls plus and 0.40Ls per kilometre between midnight and 6am. Bear in mind that the rising prices of petrol may greatly affect tariffs in the near future.

Riga Taxi, tel: 800 10 10, and Rīgas Taksometru Parks, tel: 800 13 13, are highly regarded and will pick up passengers anywhere in Riga. Their numbers are toll-free, and their drivers will not start the meter until you've boarded their vehicle, even if they have had to drive across town to pick you up. You can also wave down taxis on any street, but you might want to negotiate a price before getting into a vehicle. The taxis at the train and bus stations are notoriously dishonest, but the cabs at the airport are reputable. All official taxis must have a yellow number plate.

Buses, Trams and Trolleybuses

All public transport in Riga, including trams, buses, and trolleybuses, cost a flat fee of 0.20Ls for the duration of your trip, regardless of how far you travel. If you exit a tram and hop on the next available one you will have to pay for another ticket. Tickets can be purchased on board from the conductors, who run around frantically trying to check if everyone has paid in full. Trams operate from 5.24am until midnight, although night trams are in service roughly every hour on weekend nights. There are 21 different trolleybuses that one can take to destinations near and far. The same rules for trams apply to trolleybuses. For more information in English visit the Tram and Trolleybus Authority's excellent site: www.ttp.lv.

Minibuses

Often called *mikroautobusi*, or *mikriņi* for short, minibuses can provide a convenient method of transport, as they will stop at any point along a given route. However, they are slightly more expensive than trams and trolleybuses and make frequent stops – they can end up feeling like a small van packed like a tin of sardines.

Car

If you are limiting your sightseeing to the capital city, hiring a car is not necessary, as most of Riga's places of interest can be easily reached on foot or by cheap and efficient public transport. However, if you'd like to explore the countryside, then hiring a car is simple and relatively inexpensive. You must be at least 21 years of age and possess a valid driving licence, passport and major credit card. Bear in mind that some Latvians are rather irresponsible drivers, who are not above overtaking on blind turns or suddenly driving in the opposite lane of oncoming traffic to avoid a pothole. Many rural roads, which account for the vast majority of Latvia's infrastructure, are in a sad state of repair. Both **Baltic Car Lease – Sixt** (Airport; tel: 720 71 21; fax: 720 71 31; www. e-sixt.lv; and Kaļķu 28; tel: 722 40 22) and **Hertz** (Airport; tel: 720 79 80; fax: 720 79 81; www.hertz.lv; and Aspazijas bulvāris 24; tel: 722 42 23) are convenient and reputable firms.

HOURS & HOLIDAYS

Business Hours

With the exception of major shopping centres, which are usually open daily 10am–10pm, most shops are open 10am–7pm, Sat

practical information

10am–5pm and closed on Sundays. Banks and government offices are generally open weekdays 9am–5pm. Most museums are open 11am–5pm, and many are closed on Mondays and even Tuesdays. Typical office hours are 9am–5pm, excluding weekends.

Public Holidays

January 1	New Year's Day	
	Jaungads	
Moveable date	Good Friday	
	Lielā piektdiena	
Moveable date	Easter Sunday	
	Lieldienas	
Moveable date	Easter Monday	
	Otrās Lieldienas	
May 1	Labour Day	
	Strādnieku diena	
June 23–24	Midsummer celebrations	
	Līgo & Jāņi	
November 18	Independence Day 1918	
	Valsts svētki	
Dec 24–26	Christmas	
	Ziemassvētki	
Dec 31	New Year's Eve	
	Vecgada vakars	

Market Days

Groceries can be purchased at Central (Prāgas 1; open daily 8am–5pm) and Vidzeme (Matīsa 2) markets in the city centre. Flowers are for sale 24 hours a day at the market at the start of Tērbatas iela.

Left: local trams
Above: Central Market, open daily

ACCOMMODATION

Despite the fact that at least ten new hotels open in Riga each year, the city can still barely cope with the influx of visitors that has been produced by the recent tourism boom. Although finding affordable rooms in the winter won't cause you any major difficulties, you must book at least three or four months in advance if you're planning on travelling to Latvia during the peak summer months from June through August. The cost of accommodation has also skyrocketed of late, so it's not unusual for thrifty travellers to reserve rooms even six months before they set foot in the Latvian capital. The message is clear: plan ahead and don't delay.

On the bright side, the quality and amenities in hotels has improved in leaps and bounds since the 1990s. Data ports for internet access, climate control, satellite television and even fitness centres have become standard in many city's hotels, and most staff at even the most forlorn two-star motel can speak at least three languages including English.

Whether it's boutique hotels with cutting-edge design, tourist-class hotels that can provide enough room for 1,000 guests, or simply a quiet family-run bed and breakfast you're after, Riga has something for everyone. Backpackers can also take advantage of a host of new, European-style youth hostels that have mushroomed in Old Riga. To book accommodation online, visit one of the following local websites: www.allhotels.lv or www.inyourpocket.com.

Key to price ranges:

$$$$$	over 100Ls
$$$$	70–100Ls
$$$	50–70Ls
$$	30–50Ls
$	under 30Ls

Expensive

Ainavas Boutique Hotel
Peldu 23
Tel: 781 43 16
Fax: 781 43 17
www.ainavas.lv
This is by far Riga's loveliest boutique hotel. Housed in a medieval building on the edge of Old Riga, each of its 22 rooms is decorated in a different style, taking the tone and colour from a photograph of a Latvian landscape or *ainava* hung above the bed. A stay during the week is recommended, as guests have reported noise from a neighbouring nightclub at the weekends. $$$$$

Grand Palace Hotel
Pils 12
Tel: 704 40 00
Fax: 704 40 04
www.schlossle-hotels.com
The words 'grand' and 'palace' certainly aren't exaggerations. Every guest is pampered like royalty, which is perhaps the reason that Sting and Catherine Deneuve chose to stay here when they visited Riga. Rooms are lavishly decorated and include all of the amenities one would expect from a world-class hotel. There are also two upmarket restaurants. $$$$$

Hotel Bergs
Elizabetes 83–85 (Berga bazārs)
Tel: 777 09 00
Fax: 777 09 40
www.hotelbergs.com
Located in the middle of Riga's chicest outdoor shopping plaza, Bergs is so luxurious that it only offers suites decorated by Riga's finest interior designers. Named one of the top 100 hotels in the world by Condé Nast Traveler, it not only offers excellent accommodation, but also the city's finest gourmet restaurant. *See also page 77.* $$$$$

Hotel de Rome
Kaļķu 28
Tel: 708 76 00
Fax: 708 76 06
www.derome.lv
One of the first upmarket hotels to emerge in Riga after the fall of communism, on Old Riga's central pedestrian street near the Freedom Monument. Luxurious rooms on several floors surround a central atrium, and every imaginable amenity is available to its guests, including one of the best restaurants in the city with incredible panoramic views of the Opera and Canal Park. $$$$$

Radisson-SAS Daugava
Kuģu 24
Tel: 706 11 11
Fax: 706 11 00
www.radissonsas.com
Although some complain that the Radisson was built on the wrong side of the river, its location on the left bank affords its guests unparalleled views of Old Riga's ancient

Top: Orangerie, Grand Palace Hotel
Left: Hotel Bergs

skyline. Other perks include a large swimming pool and two excellent restaurants, not to mention spacious, modern rooms only a short walk from the city's best sights. **$$$$$**

Reval Hotel Rīdzene
Reimersa 1
Tel: 732 44 33
Fax: 732 26 00
www.revalhotels.com
Built in the 1980s as a hotel for the elite of Soviet society, this building illustrates the USSR's lack of appreciation of spectacular views. Although the hotel is flanked by scenic parks on either side, most of the rooms look onto the buildings to its right and left. They have however been completely renovated and include air-conditioning, internet access and tasteful interior design. There's an excellent restaurant housed in a glass pyramid. **$$$$$**

Upmarket
Centra
Audēju 1
Tel: 722 64 41
Fax: 750 32 81
www.centra.lv
Located in the heart of Old Riga, this excellent hotel offers cutting-edge minimalist design in its spacious rooms and some of the friendliest staff in the city. Spectacular views of the busy cobblestoned streets and the red terracotta tiles of the old city's roofs are in stark contrast to its modern, uncluttered interiors. Breakfast is served downstairs in a renovated brick cellar with vaulted ceilings. Great value for money. **$$$**

Hotel Gutenbergs
Doma laukums 1
Tel: 781 40 90
Fax: 750 33 26
www.gutenbergs.lv
Only a few steps away from the largest house of worship in the Baltics, Dome Cathedral, Gutenbergs would be a popular place to stay even if it didn't offer luxurious accommodation. Luckily it does. Rooms in the older wing are cosier, with rustic interiors that incorporate original elements of the building, while rooms in the newer section have a more modern feel. The penthouse restaurant with unparalleled views of the square is not to be missed in the summer months. **$$$**

Konventa Sēta
Kalēju 9–11
Tel: 708 75 01
Fax: 708 75 15
www.konventa.lv

Above: Ainavas Boutique Hotel

The Convent Yard is part of the original fortress that protected crusading Germans from fierce Liv and Latvian tribes at the beginning of the 13th century. A complex of renovated medieval buildings, it is now home to this cosy hotel as well as dozens of shops and cafés. Although some rooms are delightful, with original oak beams and exposed brick walls, many others are plain and generic, so be specific about the kind of accommodation you're looking for before booking a room here. $$$

Metropole
Aspazijas bulv. 36–38
Tel: 722 54 11
Fax: 721 61 40
www.metropole.lv
The Metropole is the oldest continuously running hotel in Riga, and has been catering to the city's guests only a stone's throw from the Opera House since 1871. Standard rooms aren't the most spacious but include every amenity one would expect from a four-star hotel. Fitness and business centres and an upmarket restaurant serving international cuisine are also at your disposal. Excellent views too. $$$$

Reval Hotel Latvija
Elizabetes 55
Tel: 777 22 22
Fax: 777 22 21
www.revalhotels.com
An In-Tourist hotel during the Soviet era and the only place that foreigners were allowed to stay in Riga, the city's largest hotel has been completely renovated and is now impressive even by Western standards. Nearly 400 rooms with incredible views are available on 27 floors, as well as a top-storey bar, upmarket restaurant, fitness centre and top-notch conference facilities. $$$$

Viesturs
Mucenieku 5
Tel: 735 60 60
Fax: 735 60 61
www.hotelviesturs.lv
This cosy boutique hotel on a quiet cobble-stoned street in Old Riga offers a variety of rooms, each decorated in a different fashion. While some are tasteful with all of the standard amenities, others lean towards the garish end of the style spectrum. The suite has the added benefit of a sauna, hot tub and private penthouse terrace with excellent views. $$$

Moderate

Forums
Vaļņu 45
Tel: 781 46 80
Fax: 781 46 82
www.hotelforums.lv
Nearly all of the rooms of this centrally located hotel are identical, with maroon and gold furnishings as well as satellite television, phone, writing desk and en suite with baths. Suites with balconies are also available as well as one room with its own sauna. Reasonable rates in Old Riga are scarce, so book this hotel well in advance of your trip. $$

Hotel Sesame
Mūkusalas 56
Tel: 762 13 10
Fax: 762 13 10
www.hotelsesame.lv
What this cosy hotel on the left bank of the river lacks in location, it more than makes

Left: Old Riga

up for in its inexpensive rates and family-style atmosphere. Doubles are pretty spacious and are tastefully designed, with amenities including cable television, telephone, writing desk and private bathrooms. The ground-floor restaurant offers a pleasant garden terrace in the summer and specialises in cuisine from the Caucasus Mountains and Central Asia. **$$**

Kolonna Hotel Riga
Tirgoņu 9
Tel: 735 82 54
Fax: 735 82 55
reservationriga@kolonna.com
If you are fortunate enough to book a room at this stylish hotel, you will be rewarded with excellent service, incredibly low prices, given its location next to Dome Square, and tastefully decorated rooms, with standard amenities such as satellite television and private bathrooms. Breakfast is served in a trendy chocolate shop on the ground floor. **$$**

Laine
Skolas 11
Tel: 728 88 16
Fax: 728 76 58
www.laine.lv
This delightful hotel occupies the top three floors of an Art Nouveau building in the city centre; it offers tastefully decorated rooms with the usual amenities as well as more spartan rooms with shared showers and toilets for budget travellers. Seasonal attractions include a summer penthouse terrace restaurant and a winter fireplace. **$$–$$$**

Radi un Draugi
Mārstaļu 1/3
Tel: 782 02 00
Fax: 782 02 02
www.draugi.lv
Owned by a British-Latvian exile organisation, this hotel, whose name means 'Family and Friends', was originally created to offer reasonably priced accommodation for the visiting Latvian diaspora and still lives up to its commitment to providing relatively inexpensive rooms. Book well in advance, as budget Old Riga hotels often fill up quickly. **$$**

Bed & Breakfast
Barons B&B
K. Barona 25
Tel: 910 59 39
www.baronsbb.com
This small bed and breakfast is owned and operated by Australian-Latvians who personally greet their guests and offer them a complimentary beer to boot. Rooms have hardwood floors, beautifully tiled Art Nouveau fireplaces and great views of one of Riga's busiest streets below. Inexpensive hostel-style dormitory rooms also available. **$$**

KB
K. Barona 37
Tel: 731 23 23
Fax: 731 69 53
www.kbhotel.lv
KB are the initials of Latvia's illustrious collector of folksongs, Krišjānis Barons, after whom the street below is named. He is also the ancestor of the owner of this cosy bed and breakfast, which offers spacious rooms with hardwood floors, cable television and private bathrooms. A communal kitchen and computer with internet access are also available, but if you're not ready to climb a lot of stairs, you might consider alternate accommodation. **$–$$**

Lenz Bed and Breakfast
Lenču 2
Tel: 733 33 43
Fax: 733 13 78
www.lenz.lv
Only a few minutes' walk from some of the city's most stunning Art Nouveau architecture, this ever-expanding bed and breakfast has converted several apartments in one building into bright, spacious rooms with shared showers and toilets. A communal kitchen is available on each floor as well as a computer with free internet access. **$$**

Camping
Riga City Camping
Ķīpsalas 8
Tel: 706 50 00
www.bt1.lv/camping
Riga City Camping offers cheap alternative accommodation only a short trip across the Vanšu Bridge from the old town. It also rents

Most backpackers have never seen such opulent surroundings apart from the museums they visit on their travels. Dormitory rooms in this historic medieval building include luxuriously high ceilings with dangling chandeliers, and the common room – with a television and couches – looks like it belongs in a palace. No curfew. **$**

Riga Old Town Hostel
Vaļņu 43
Tel: 722 34 06
www.rigaoldtownhostel.lv
Although several new hostels have sprouted up around the old town of late, they can't hold a candle to this cosy Lithuanian-run hostel, which provides more than just accommodation for financially challenged backpackers. Each guest can take advantage of personal safes, free washing machines and internet access, a sauna, communal kitchen and a great pub that is the perfect place to meet fellow travellers. The staff can also arrange visas to Latvia's neighbouring Slavic nations. **$**

HEALTH & EMERGENCIES

Hygiene/General Health
Although tap water is safe to use for brushing your teeth, bottled water is recommended for drinking. Local mineral waters such as *Mangaļi* and *Rāmava* are widely available and often extremely inexpensive.

Pharmacies
Generic versions of many common over-the-counter drugs are available at the majority of pharmacies or *aptiekas* in Latvia. Unfortunately, poor economic circumstances often encourage pharmacists and their staff to turn a blind eye to sales of certain medications such as antibiotics and even *Viagra* without a prescription. Vecpilsētas aptieka, Audēju 20, tel: 721 33 40, is a 24-hour pharmacy in Old Riga.

Medical/Dental Services
If you're planning on visiting the Latvian countryside for an extended period of time, a vaccination against tick-borne encephalitis is recommended. If, like most visitors,

tents, barbecues and bicycles and provides a laundry service for only 2Ls. **$**

Countryside Accommodation
Lauku Ceļotājs
Kuģu 11 (entrance from Uzvaras)
Tel: 761 76 00
Fax: 783 00 41
www.celotajs.lv
The Country Traveller offers bed and breakfast-style accommodation, often with fireplaces and saunas, in the Latvian countryside in a wide variety of locations, and prices are often ridiculously inexpensive. Activities such as fishing, hunting, swimming, canoeing and horse riding can usually be arranged. **$**

Hostels
Riga Backpackers
Mārstaļu 6
Tel: 722 99 22
Fax: 722 10 23
www.riga-backpackers.com

Above: the 1924 Laima Clock (Laimas pulkstenis), a favourite Riga meeting place

you only intend on visiting Riga and cities outside the capital, a vaccination shouldn't be necessary.

An international insurance policy or at least travel insurance are always recommended, but medication, minor emergency treatments and diagnostic tests are relatively cheap in Riga. The following are reputable emergency service facilities with English-speaking doctors and dentists: ARS (Skolas 5; tel: 720 10 01) and Diplomatic Service Medical Centre (Elizabetes 57; tel: 722 99 42; fax: 728 94 13).

Crime/Trouble

Riga is no more dangerous than many European capitals. If you do have the misfortune of becoming a victim of crime, it will no doubt be petty theft or pickpocketing. Mind your wallet and other belongings in trams and trolleybuses, at the Central Market and especially the pedestrian tunnels that connect Old Riga to the train and bus stations. Muggings are rare, but expatriates have been beaten up and robbed in the early hours of the morning on their way home from clubs, so the prudent choice would be to take a cab back to your hotel if you've had a lot to drink.

Street children can be a nuisance and sadly many use the spare change given to them to sniff glue or play arcade games. If you'd truly like to help poor children, offer to buy them food. Beware of amber touts selling their often artificial wares from plastic bags. Souvenir stalls and shops are a much better option, and you're guaranteed to get the genuine article.

Police

Local police are often accused of being apathetic and corrupt, but higher wages have lessened bribe taking, and visitors should not hesitate to ask a policeman for help if needed. Bear in mind that the police are within their rights to detain inebriated people deemed nuisances to the public, even though foreign nationals are rarely approached. However, drunken troublemakers can be forced to spend the night in the drunk tank, an experience not soon forgotten. To call the police dial 02 toll free or 112 for an emergency operator.

Toilets

Most public toilets throughout the city are in a sad state. If you're looking for a little piece of the Soviet past, then pay the 0.10Ls entrance fee and descend into the depths of filthy tiled cellars that reek of urine, ammonia and other things better left unmentioned. The only exceptions are the toilets at the train station, but restaurants and hotel lobbies are still your best option. Men's and women's toilets are usually designated with a triangle pointing down or up, respectively.

COMMUNICATIONS & NEWS

Post

There seem to be very few services that Latvian post offices don't offer. You can wire money, send letters and packages, pay your electric or phone bill, buy magazines or send faxes. The main post office is located next to the train station (Stacijas laukums 1; tel: 701 88 04; www.pasts.lv).

Telephone

Latvia's telecommunications system has been completely overhauled and, with the exception of a few distant rural towns, is now state-of-the-art digital. All telephone

Right: wi-fi surfing

can be bought at most kiosks and shops around town and at the airport. Instructions are available in English when you purchase the card.

Media

Most major world newspapers, including the *Financial Times*, *Wall Street Journal Europe*, *Herald Tribune* and *USA Today*, are available at Narvesen shops and kiosks. For local news in English, buy a copy of the weekly *Baltic Times* newspaper. Of the many local city guides available throughout the Latvian capital, the highly acclaimed *Riga In Your Pocket* is by far the best choice, offering witty, independent restaurant, nightlife and museum reviews as well as practical information, maps and an entertainment schedule.

TV and Radio

Local cable packages include the BBC World Service and CNN, as well as a few music and sports channels in English. Riga does not have any English-language radio stations, but you can turn your dial to 100.5 for the BBC World Service.

Wireless Internet

If you have a laptop and would like to check your email or surf the web, many cafés, bars and restaurants sell wireless internet cards. Look for the yellow wi-fi sticker at participating establishments.

USEFUL INFORMATION

Travellers with Disabilities

Sadly, there are very few hotels, restaurants or museums that are disabled-friendly. Although Latvia is now a member of the EU, it is still one of the poorest nations in the Union, and improving roads often takes precedence over bringing public buildings up to international standards.

Children

There are not that many options for children's entertainment in a country with a mortality rate that is higher than its birth rate. The restaurants Vairāk Saules (Dzirnavu 60; tel: 728 28 78) and Spotikačs (Antonijas 12; tel:

numbers consist of seven digits, although this will change to eight at the end of 2006. One number will precede all landlines, and another will be added to the beginning of all mobile numbers.

To call anywhere in Latvia from within the country just dial the seven-digit number. To call Latvia from abroad, dial your country's international dialling code (00 within Europe) and Latvia's country code 371, followed by the number. To call abroad from Latvia dial 00, the country code and then the number.

Public phones are available all over the city, but a phone card is required to operate them. Cards can be purchased at most kiosks and shops, which display the *telekarte* sign. Phone cards can be bought for 2, 5 and 10Ls. You can also use a credit card to make a call from a phone booth. Simply follow the instructions in English inside.

Mobile Phones

If you'd like to avoid exorbitant roaming charges while in Latvia, pre-paid SIM cards

Above: view over the city
Right: a treat for the kids

750 59 55) offer special recreation areas for kids, with lego, games and colouring books, while the stylish cocktail bar B-Bārs (Doma laukums 2; tel: 722 88 42) provides a supervised game room. The kitsch Lido atpūtas centrs (Krasta 76; tel: 750 44 20; http://ac.lido.lv) is a giant self-service restaurant on three floors that also operates an amusement park with children's rides, slides and an ice-skating rink in the winter.

The Leļļu teātris (Puppet Theatre; K. Barona 16–18; tel: 728 54 18; www.puppet.lv) and Rīgas cirks (Riga Circus; Merķeļa 4; tel: 722 02 72; www.circusriga.lv) are also good options to stave off pre-pubescent boredom. Similarly, Rīgas zooloģiskais dārzs (Riga Zoo; Meža prospekts 1; tel: 751 84 09; www.rigazoo.lv), with its lions, bears, tigers and crocodiles, never fails to impress both young and old.

A short trip to Jūrmala promises a day of aquatic action at Līvu Akvaparks water park (Lielupe, Vienības gatve 36; tel: 775 56 40; www.akvaparks.lv), where there are water slides, indoor and outdoor pools, a tubing river and other attractions, not to mention an excellent restaurant and bar for adults. During the summer months kids can ride small motorcars, jump around on inflatable attractions or do somersaults on trampolines in Wöhrmann and Esplanade parks.

Maps

Local maps can be obtained at tourist information centres and at the Jāņa Sēta map shop (Elizabetes 83–85; tel: 724 08 92; www.kartes.lv). Maps are also available in the majority of city guides distributed around town, including *Riga In Your Pocket* (www.inyourpocket.com).

Bookshops

For the widest selection of travel guides in the Baltic States visit the Jāņa Sēta map shop (Elizabetes 83–85; tel: 724 08 92; www.kartes.lv). A small selection of English-language books can be purchased at the following shops:
• Jāņa Rozes grāmatnīca, K. Barona 5, tel: 728 42 88, www.jr.lv.
• Globuss, Vaļņu 26, tel: 722 69 57.
• Valters un Rapa, Aspazijas 24, tel: 760 16 42.

LANGUAGE

Latvian is a Baltic language similar only to Lithuanian. It is *not* Slavic. Of all the continent's Indo-European tongues, modern Latvian and Lithuanian are the closest languages to Sanskrit, and many words are still remarkably similar to their ancient roots. A good deal of Latvians over the age of 50 speak German, while members of the younger generation are often eager to show off their knowledge of English. Any attempt by a foreigner to speak Latvian is often greeted with grateful surprise.

One curious aspect of the Latvian lan-

guage is its relentless effort to change foreign names and places to fit its grammatical usage. Major urban centres such as New York and Munich become *Ņujorka* and *Minhene*, while heads of state and film stars become *Džordžs Bušs* and *Breds Pits* in Latvian. An easy rule of thumb for people is that an *s*, *is* or *š* is almost always added to the end of male names and an *a* or *e* is added the end of female names.

Another peculiarity of the language is that only place names and proper names are capitalised, so the Latvians are *latvieši*, the English are *angļi*, Saturday is *sestdiena* and July is *jūlijs*.

SPORT

Bowling
Bowlero, Lielirbes 27, tel: 780 46 00, www.bowlero.lv.
Zelta boulinga centrs, Uzvaras 2–4, tel: 761 07 07.

Football
Matches in Riga in this increasingly popular sport are held at the Skonto Stadium, E. Melngaiļa 1a, www.fcskonto,lv.

Golf
Courses include **OZO**, Mielgrāvja 16, tel: 739 43 99, www.ozogolf.lv. and **Viesturi**, tel: 644 43 90, www.golfsviesturi.lv.

Tennis
Enri, Kalnciema 207, tel: 770 55 88, www.enri.lv.

Shooting Galleries
Reast, Daugavgrīvas 23a, tel: 760 17 05.

Swimming Pools
Līvu Akvaparks, Lielupe, Vienības gatve 36, tel: 775 56 40, www.akvaparks.lv.
Technogym Wellness Centre, Kuģu 24, tel: 706 11 24.

USEFUL ADDRESSES

Tourist Offices
Riga offers three tourist-information centres providing maps, brochures, practical advice and hotel reservations.
Rātslaukums 6, tel: 703 79 00, open daily 9am–7pm, www.rigatourism.com.
Prāgas 1 (Bus Station), tel: 722 05 55, open daily 9am–7pm.
Stacijas 2 (Train Station), tel: 723 38 15, open daily 10am–6.30pm.

Other centres include:
Latvian Tourist Information Centre; Smilšu 4, tel: 722 46 64, open daily 9am–7pm.
Jūrmala Tourist Information Centre, Lienes 5, tel: 714 79 00, open Mon–Fri

Above: shouting for the Latvian football team
Right: taking a break from the festivities

9am–7pm, Sat 10am–5pm, Sun 10am–3pm, www.jurmala.lv.
Sigulda Tourist Information Centre, Valdemāra 1a, tel: 797 13 35, open daily May–Oct 10am–7pm, Nov–Apr 10am–5pm, www.sigulda.lv.
Bauska District Tourist Information Centre, Rātslaukums 1, tel: 392 37 97, open May–Sept 9am–6pm, Sat–Sun 10.30am–3.30pm, Oct–Apr Mon–Fri 9am–5pm, www.tourism.bauska.lv.

Latvian Tourist Offices Abroad
United Kingdom
Latvian Tourism Information Bureau in London: 72 Queensborough Terrace, London, tel: +44 (0)20-7229 82 71.

Germany
Baltikum Tourismus Zentrale – Estland, Lettland, Litauen Katharinenstrasse 19–20, 10711 Berlin, tel: +49 (0)30-8900 9091, www. gobaltic.de.

Finland
Latvian Tourism Information Bureau in Helsinki, Mariankatu 8B, 00170 Helsinki, tel: +358 92 78 47 74, fax: +358 968 742 650.

Sweden
Latvian Tourism Information Centre in Stockholm, Vattugatan 7, 11152 Stockholm, tel: +46 820 81 50, fax: +46 820 81 54.

Sightseeing Tours
The tourist information centre on Rātslaukums can help organise tours of Riga as well as day trips to the Latvian countryside.
Amber Way, tel: 652 08 06, swww.sightseeing.lv

Latvia Tours, Kaļķu 8, tel: 708 50 01 www.latviatours.lv

Embassies
Australia Contact the UK embassy
Canada
Baznīcas 20–22, tel: 781 39 45, fax: 781 39 60, www.dfait-maeci.qc.ca.
New Zealand Contact the UK embassy
Republic of Ireland
Brīvības iela 54, tel: 702 25 222, fax: 702 25 223
UK
Alunāna 5, tel: 777 47 00, fax: 777 47 07, www.britain.lv
USA
Raiņa bulvāris 7, tel: 703 62 00, fax: 782 00 47, www. usembassy.lv

FURTHER READING

Insight Guide Baltic States, Apa Publications, 2005. A fully illustrated guide providing in-depth essays, detailed coverage of the sights, excellent maps and accessible, up-to-date practical information
Art Nouveau in Riga, Silvija Grosa, Jumava, Riga, 2003. An in-depth explanation of Riga's Art Nouveau heritage.
We Sang Through Tears, edited and translated by Astrid Sics, Jānis Roze Publishers, Riga, 1999. A compilation of moving first-hand recollections by Latvians sent to Siberia.
The Merry Baker of Riga, Boris Zemtzov, Stanford Oak Press, Washington DC, 2004. An American entrepreneur's humorous account of starting a business in Latvia during the chaos that followed independence in the early 1990s.

practical information

ACKNOWLEDGEMENTS

Photography	**Anna Mockford & Nick Bonetti/Apa**
and	
91	**Ainavas Boutique Hotel**
70, 82	**allOver photography/Alamy**
15t, 15b	**gettyimages**
42	**gettyimages/stone**
90t	**Grand Palace Hotel**
90b	**Hotel Berg**
27, 52, 69, 79, 81, 84, 96, 97, 98, 99	**Latvian Tourist Association**
32/33	**Lyle Lawson**
14	**Reekst**
10, 13	**Riga Museum of History and Navigation**
Cover	**CapitalCity Images/Alamy**
Cartography	**Phoenix Mapping**

© APA Publications GmbH & Co. Verlag KG Singapore Branch, Singapore

INDEX